T0346513

"It's hard to beat George Marsden as a guide to Jonathan Edwards—and this gem of a book will be treasured by thousands who know or will discover exactly what I mean. It sparkles brightly with profound Christian wisdom from the past interpreted for modern-day readers with clarity and a large helping of simple—though also deeply learned—Christian common sense."

Douglas A. Sweeney, dean of the Beeson Divinity School at Samford University

"In this brief but wonderfully written appreciation of Jonathan Edwards by prize-winning scholar George Marsden, readers encounter an Edwards meant for twenty-first-century believers. In place of emphasizing Edwards's celebrated but difficult philosophical treatises like *Freedom of the Will* or *The Nature of True Virtue*, Marsden offers an insightful overview of Edwards's classic *A Treatise Concerning Religious Affections*, celebrated by William James as America's first religious psychology. In Marsden's hands, readers learn to understand Edwards's signs of saving faith in terms as relevant to today as they were in the eighteenth century. In the process, they see a new meaning of the Enlightenment grounded less in 'laws' of nature than in a system of personal interrelationships governed by a caring, sovereign God."

Harry Stout, Jonathan Edwards Professor Emeritus of American Religious History, Yale University

"A remarkable book that renders Jonathan Edwards highly accessible to twenty-first-century evangelicals. Marsden wonderfully brings together a lifetime of reflection on American religious history and decades of work on Edwards to reveal the ways Edwards's powerful theological vision and penetrating spiritual theology can practically contribute to the renewal of the church today. *An Infinite Fountain of Light* is an outstanding example of how history and biography inspire, convey a sense of wisdom, and positively inform our present."

Robert W. Caldwell III, professor of church history at Southwestern Baptist Theological Seminary

"In a culture still in thrall to the ideals of Benjamin Franklin, George Marsden calls American evangelicals back to Jonathan Edwards's coruscating vision of divine beauty."

Amy Plantinga Pauw, Louisville Presbyterian Seminary

"I am delighted to recommend *An Infinite Fountain of Light*. This book is an engaging and practical consideration of what Jonathan Edwards has to say to the twenty-first century. With characteristic insight, clarity, and Christian wisdom, George Marsden guides readers through the thought of one of Christianity's most brilliant and challenging theologians."

Thomas S. Kidd, research professor of church history at Midwestern Baptist Theological Seminary

"At a time when evangelicals—and Christians generally—seem unsure of themselves, George Marsden offers us Jonathan Edwards as a fixed star in the firmament and encourages us to navigate our twenty-first-century voyage with sextants set on Northampton. Here Marsden distills the essence of his earlier Bancroft award–winning biography of Edwards and reflects on issues such as worldview, discernment, rightly ordered love, and a faithful yet winsome approach to Christian social engagement. What Marsden brings to light is just what Edwards did, namely everything. Nothing looks quite the same when it is viewed in the light of God's reality. This culminating work by an outstanding historian of American religion deserves a wide readership."

Michael McClymond, professor of modern Christianity at Saint Louis University

"Jonathan Edwards is the greatest theologian in American history, and George Marsden is the greatest historian of American Christianity writing today. In this lyrical book, Marsden does the hard work of retrieval for us all, finding insights in Edwards's work that can guide believers in the twenty-first century. *An Infinite Fountain of Light* is a gift to the whole church from one of its most thoughtful members."

Timothy Larsen, McManis Professor of Christian Thought at Wheaton College

An
INFINITE
FOUNTAIN
of LIGHT

An

INFINITE
FOUNTAIN
of LIGHT

JONATHAN EDWARDS *for*
the TWENTY-FIRST CENTURY

GEORGE MARSDEN

IVP Academic

An imprint of InterVarsity Press
Downers Grove, Illinois

InterVarsity Press
P.O. Box 1400 | Downers Grove, IL 60515-1426
ivpress.com | email@ivpress.com

©2023 by George Mish Marsden

All rights reserved. No part of this book may be reproduced in any form without written permission from InterVarsity Press.

InterVarsity Press® is the publishing division of InterVarsity Christian Fellowship/USA®. For more information, visit intervarsity.org.

All Scripture quotations, unless otherwise indicated, are from the King James Version, which is in the public domain.

The publisher cannot verify the accuracy or functionality of website URLs used in this book beyond the date of publication.

Cover design: David Fassett
Interior design: Jeanna Wiggins

ISBN 978-1-5140-0662-7 (hardcover) | ISBN 978-1-5140-0663-4 (digital)

Printed in the United States of America ∞

Library of Congress Cataloging-in-Publication Data
A catalog record for this book is available from the Library of Congress.

29 28 27 26 25 24 23 | 12 11 10 9 8 7 6 5 4 3 2 1

To Mark and Maggie Noll

CONTENTS

ACKNOWLEDGMENTS

THIS BOOK HAS been a long time in the making. It started out as five presentations for the Stone Lectures at Princeton Theological Seminary in 2008. I am very grateful to the Stone Lectures committee and the seminary for their support and fine hospitality. After that I offered variations on some of those lectures at other venues. Several of the chapters of the present volume have some resemblance to the original; the rest of the book is new. Some of the themes have arisen from my teaching about Edwards for many years, including at Calvin Theological Seminary over the past decade. I would like to thank students and colleagues whom I have worked with over the years for refining my understandings. I am especially grateful to my friends and former students Kenneth P. Minkema and Harry S. Stout for making the Works of Jonathan Edwards project and the Yale Jonathan Edwards Center and Online Archives into such valuable and comprehensive resources. I am also grateful for the semester I had in 2017 at the Biola Center for Christian Thought, where we were trying to understand humility. There, with the help of wonderful colleagues, I developed some of the themes in this book.

I am also indebted to Derek Schuurman for recommending his editor at IVP Academic, Jon Boyd. And now I am especially grateful to Jon Boyd for his excellent editorial help. I also wish to thank the entire IVP editorial team for their impressively high quality work.

A PERSON *of* HIS TIME *for* OUR TIME

The next best thing to being wise oneself is
to live in a circle of those who are.

C. S. LEWIS

CHRISTIANS IN EVERY era need to pause once in a while to get their bearings. Though we belong to churches that give us some good guidance, that advice must compete with bewildering numbers of other voices we hear during the week. It is as though we are hiking in a land only half familiar to us, and we are confronted with many unmarked, poorly marked, or—increasingly—wrongly marked turns. So we may feel we are losing our way in the face of perplexing and enticing options. Or we may feel that the denominations or Christian movements that we have followed are themselves losing their way and are offering us inadequate directions. And even if we believe that we are on essentially the right path, it may be helpful to reconnoiter once in a while to see if we can be wiser in the ways that we proceed.

As one who has spent many years trying to understand the interrelationships between Christianity and American culture, I see the calling of a Christian historian as helping us step back in order to gain perspective on where we are by looking at how we got there. That is not the most important calling within the body of Christ, but it is one of the valuable functions from which I believe the whole body can benefit. If we think of Christians today as being part of a fellowship on a great quest, such as in *The Lord of the Rings*, then we might view historians and other cultural observers as comparable to some Hobbits who have been assigned the task of keeping careful records of where we have been. They can help see where and why we have made some wrong turns, or correct ones. That can help the whole company as it makes future choices. Unfortunately our maps give us only the general direction to our destination, and we can only guess at the contours of the territory that lies ahead. And we are only Hobbits. We need wise leaders like Gandalf and Aragorn to interpret the clues from the guidelines we have been given and to lead us in the right direction. So I see my contribution as twofold. First, as a historian, I hope I can, in the light of our past successes and failures, help identify what are some of the greatest cultural challenges for Christians today in negotiating their way through the contemporary world. Second, as a Christian who knows how difficult it can be to meet those challenges, I have learned to look to the wisdom of some of the guides who have proven reliable in many cultural settings and so can help us to know where to turn in our own.

Jonathan Edwards is among those mentors who present some striking insights that I have found especially helpful in my ongoing personal quest. So I offer this little book in the hope of sharing that guidance with others.

Looking to the most profound insights of Christians from another era can be an especially helpful way to gain perspective on our own needs in our own era. Edwards lived in a time differing greatly from our own, when people assumed some outlooks we may find puzzling or simply wrong. Yet precisely because Edwards lived in such a radically different era, he can help us to see our present situation in a new light. One of the things that the study of history can help us recognize is the degree to which people are shaped and sometimes blinded by the prevailing assumptions of their age and culture. The most important implication of that observation is that people in our own age are not exceptions to that rule. And that includes us. Once we are alert to the danger of being blinded by assumptions of our own time, we can attempt to identify those assumptions and to assess critically which are blinding and which may be valid. For those purposes, in can be especially helpful to view our times in the light of the wisdom from other times.

In studying the Christian past, I have found Jonathan Edwards especially helpful both in challenging assumptions of our own age and in offering invigorating guidance in my own quest to follow Christ. Edwards is not, of course, alone in this regard. Any one of scores of great Christian saints of the past or present might serve as comparably wise guides. For instance, I have been helped or inspired at various times by Augustine, J. S. Bach, Pascal, Kierkegaard, the Niebuhr brothers, Martin Luther King Jr., J. R. R. Tolkien, and C. S. Lewis, as well as many other past and more recent writers. It happens, though, that my interest in Edwards led to me study him in depth and to publish two biographies about him. So I have had more opportunity to think about how his best insights are helpful for my own faith. That study also reminds me of my own limitations. It is far easier to articulate the grandeur of Edwards's theological vision than it is to begin to respond to it as one should. I suppose such a strong sense of inadequacy is what anyone should expect when trying to understand and to follow God's Word and God's ways in the world. Still, I feel that inadequacy acutely in the presence of the grandeur of the Christian vision and in facing the challenges of following its implications.

In thinking about Edwards in relation to other great Christian thinkers, I have been particularly struck, for instance, by some of the parallels with C. S. Lewis, someone else whom I have been privileged to write about and whom I will invoke occasionally. Some readers might find that pairing counterintuitive. Edwards and Lewis are so different in so many ways. Lewis is a theological essentialist who presents "mere Christianity" as "those beliefs that have been common to all Christians at all times."[1] In doing so, he is drawing on the Christian mainstream that flows though Augustine. Edwards is a theological maximalist who attempts to work out in detail all of the implications of classic Christian belief. He is explicitly Reformed, which means that he draws most directly on a couple of centuries—since the time of John Calvin—of Protestant theological elaboration of the classic Augustinian heritage. That is a reminder that much of what is profound in Edwards is not unique to him. But I invoke Lewis as a particularly useful counterpart to Edwards. Lewis makes a point of not being original. Rather, he says, he is trying to draw on the most common

---

[1] C. S. Lewis, *Mere Christianity*, The Complete C. S. Lewis Signature Classics (New York: HarperOne, 2002), 6.

essentials of the Christian theological tradition throughout the ages. So I find Lewis's breadth in his inclusive and nonjudgmental reaching out to all sorts of traditional Christians a nice balance to the strict dogmatism that sometimes accompanies Edwards's astonishing depth of insights.

One of Lewis's most helpful insights is that most Christian theologians need translators. With that principle in mind, he recommended that every examination in theology "ought to include a passage from some standard theological work for translation into the vernacular."[2] If you cannot explain a theological principle in terms that ordinary Christians can understand, then you probably do not understand the doctrine very well yourself.

Edwards particularly needs translators. Though he was sometimes a remarkably effective preacher, most often that effectiveness had to do with his personal intensity in addressing New England audiences who were well schooled in Reformed theology and used to formal expositions. And his theological and ethical treatises were addressed to highly educated clergy and others with philosophical training who could follow subtle and complex arguments. Much of what he wrote in his extensive private notebooks is even more philosophical and obscure. Furthermore, he wrote in an eighteenth-century idiom that is sometimes hard to follow in our time. In each of these modes of writing, he sometimes came up with brilliant and even beautiful passages. But those are the gems that may be extracted only through a lot of deep mining.

---

[2] C. S. Lewis, "God in the Dock," *God in the Dock,* ed. Walter Hooper (Grand Rapids, MI: Eerdmans, 1970), 243.

So I view one of my roles in this volume as to be a translator of Edwards. As a Christian layperson who has been helped by many of his insights, I can in turn try to help others discover and appreciate those insights. And as someone who has studied Christianity in American culture, I can also suggest how those insights speak particularly to our cultural settings today.

Some aspects of Edwards's thought, it must be acknowledged, are not at all helpful. Sometimes he carries his insights too far. And sometimes he gets off on a wrong track. That is most glaringly evident, for instance, in his interpretation of biblical prophecies. Adopting a then-current interpretive framework, he believed that the key to understanding recent history was that the Roman Catholic Church was the antichrist spoken of in the Scriptures. Given that premise, Protestants could interpret biblical prophecies as predicting that the papal powers—such as the Roman Catholic nations of France and Spain that were often at war with Great Britain and threatened New World Protestantism—would eventually be defeated. After that, as Edwards interpreted Scripture, true Christianity would spread remarkably, and the world would rapidly improve. The last era in human history would be a golden age lasting a thousand years, the "millennium" in Scripture. And probably starting around the year AD 2000, at the end of the golden millennial age, Christ would return. This was what is now called a postmillennial view. A great mind working from wrong premises can produce spectacular errors.

So it should be clear that my outlook in these reflections is not at all that just because Edwards says something, we must pay attention to it or learn from it. Rather, recognizing that Edwards, like the rest of us, had his share of shortcomings, I hope to offer readers the best of Edwards's insights that are most helpful today. Further, I do not present here a full account of Edwards's theology and related teachings. Many such overviews are readily available.[3] Edwards was strongly Reformed or Calvinistic. Often he elaborates aspects of that outlook in great detail. He also applies his powerful philosophical skills to trying to resolve some of its most difficult paradoxes. Many Christians, especially scholars in the Reformed heritage, find these discussions fascinating and often insightful, and I can sometimes share in such interests. However, in this book I am addressing a broader audience of Christians who have more practical concerns. The insights from Edwards presented here are filtered through my own outlook and experiences of being an American Christian in the twentieth and twenty-first centuries. His best insights are not specific to his Reformed theological tradition, even though they arise in that context. So I am confident that many who see themselves as close to that transdenominational heritage that C. S. Lewis called "mere Christianity" can benefit from Edwards. I hope and pray that readers may find many of his keen insights as invigorating as I have.

———

As the author of both a longer and a shorter biography of Edwards, I can here summarize some of the most basic insights I have to offer for understanding his life and work. Anyone who

---

[3]Michael J. McClymond and Gerald R. McDermott, *The Theology of Jonathan Edwards* (New York: Oxford University Press, 2012) is an especially helpful, comprehensive source. See also the Yale Jonathan Edwards Center website for an abundance of resources: http://edwards.yale.edu.

has read one of these (or another Edwards biography) can move on to chapter two.

Edwards lived from 1703 to 1758 and almost entirely in New England. He grew up in the village of East Windsor, Connecticut, where his father, Timothy Edwards, was the pastor. Timothy stood firmly in the old Puritan heritage. Jonathan's mother, Esther Stoddard Edwards, was the daughter of Solomon Stoddard, sometimes known as "the pope of the Connecticut River Valley" due to his dominant influence in that western Massachusetts region. Jonathan was the only boy among ten sisters, five older and five younger. Precocious and an avid reader, Jonathan began his collegiate school just before turning fourteen. He continued his studies at Yale in New Haven until 1722, when he received his MA, then the school's highest degree. During 1722 and 1723 he served as interim pastor of a Presbyterian church in the busy seaport town of New York. In 1723 he took a position as pastor of a crossroads village church in Bolton, Connecticut. Then he returned to Yale to serve as an instructor from 1724 to 1726. From there he went on to assist his grandfather, Solomon Stoddard, in Northampton, Massachusetts. In 1727 he married Sarah Pierpont, then seventeen, the daughter of a prominent New Haven pastor and someone he admired for her evident piety.

Throughout these years Jonathan's most pressing concern had to do with the state of his soul. His father emphasized regeneration, or that one needed to be "born again" by God's saving grace. Timothy Edwards also fostered some times of "awakenings," or times of religious revival, in his parish. Timothy was also an expert on the Puritan standards for determining whether one was truly converted. From his early childhood Jonathan struggled with that question, constantly gauging the state of his soul, making strict resolutions, keeping a spiritual diary, and often fearing that he was failing and deserving only of punishment. Later, when he was an established pastor and spiritual leader, he wrote an account of these struggles—a topic to which we will return. By the time he had taken up his position in Northampton and been married to Sarah, these issues seemed to have been resolved.

When Solomon Stoddard died in 1729, Jonathan became pastor of the Northampton church, where he would remain for the next twenty years. Northampton was a town of about one thousand inhabitants on the Connecticut River. Church and town were more or less coextensive, and Solomon Stoddard had been renowned for, contrary to the usual Puritan practice, not requiring accounts of conversion for church membership and participation in the sacraments. He believed that participating in the Lord's Supper might in fact sometimes be a means to conversion. Stoddard emphasized conversion itself as much as other New England pastors, and he too saw seasons of awakenings in his parish.

While still a young pastor, in the fall of 1734, Jonathan oversaw a stunning awakening in his church that lasted well into 1735. Even in this setting where churches often experienced times of spiritual renewal, this one seemed to exceed others in its intensity. And what made it especially influential was that Jonathan wrote a glowing account of it, describing how almost all the townspeople seemed concerned with the state of their souls. Titling this "A Faithful Narrative of the Surprising Work of God,"

Edwards sent his narrative to an influential pastor friend in Boston who in turn sent it on to Isaac Watts (the great hymn writer) in England. Watts enthusiastically saw to its publication. Edwards suddenly became one of the well-known promoters of revivals in an era when waves of religious renewal were beginning to build in the English-speaking world. George Whitefield and John and Charles Wesley were among the young men who were encouraged by Edwards's work and were themselves on the verge of launching monumental renewal movements.

Between 1739 and 1740 evangelist George Whitefield visited America, where his preaching, often outdoors, throughout the colonies sparked what is now called the Great Awakening. When Whitefield came to New England in 1740, he was happy to accept an invitation to visit Edwards in Northampton. Edwards, in turn, helped promote this new awakening. Particularly, he joined with some other New England clergy in traveling outside of their parishes, sometimes in teams, to hold extended awakening services in various communities. It was in such a context that in 1741 Edwards preached his famous sermon "Sinners in the Hands of an Angry God" in the village of Enfield, Connecticut. Warnings about hellfire were commonplace among almost all Christian preachers of the era, but Edwards filled this sermon with unusually vivid images depicting how precarious life was when standing on the brink of eternal damnation. His hearers in Enfield were so overcome with emotion that he could not finish. Unfortunately, in the nineteenth and twentieth centuries, when this sermon was widely anthologized, Edwards came to be better known as a hellfire preacher than for all his more positive theological insights. For many, the "Sinners" sermon is still the only thing they know about America's greatest theologian. I hope this book will fill in the picture of his much more positive appeal as an engaging teacher and mentor.

Edwards also became the most prominent apologist for the awakenings, or what became known as the "New Light" movement, writing several treatises on the subject. Critics of the awakenings, including some of Boston's most respected clergy, warned against the deceptiveness of the emotions that the awakenings generated. Edwards responded that while it was true that such reactions were sometimes superficial and deceiving, it was also true that overwhelming emotions might be appropriate responses for those who recognized the transforming grace of God in changing one's life for eternity. So to oppose the awakenings, whatever their faults, would sometimes mean to oppose the work of the Holy Spirit. Edwards recognized that telling the difference between genuine Christian conversion and its counterfeits was not an easy task. In 1746, after the awakenings had subsided, he published *A Treatise on the Religious Affections*, which remains a classic account of how to tell the difference between true Christian commitment as distinguished from hypocrisy and self-deception.

By the time Edwards was writing on this theme, developments in Northampton were beginning to cast a cloud over his work as a pastor. Small town that it was, Northampton had returned to some contentious attitudes that had long been among its tendencies. A number of church members whom Edwards had believed to be converted during the awakenings no longer evidenced the signs of true grace. And some petty resentments were now directed at Edwards and his family. Late in the decade Edwards attempted to address the issues in what proved to be a very unwise way. He proposed to reverse the lenient standards for church membership that Solomon Stoddard had instituted. Prospective church members, Edwards insisted, should be required to offer at least a minimal profession that they had been converted in a heartfelt way. Most of the congregation was up in arms at this proposal. It would have threatened not only to bar some of their adult children from communicant membership but would also then mean that some of their grandchildren would be ineligible to receive infant baptism. In 1750 the Northampton congregation voted to dismiss him as their pastor.

The next year Edwards accepted a position as a pastor and missionary to the Native Americans in Stockbridge, Massachusetts, in the mountains of the far western part of the colony. Stockbridge had been founded in the 1730s as a missionary effort by New Englanders concerned that the colonies' previous efforts to evangelize the Native Americans had largely failed. While the villagers were predominantly Mahicans, a missionary family and some others of English descent settled near them in hopes of establishing trusting relationships. Edwards already had a deep interest in Native American missions. In fact, he had published, in 1749, what became an influential spiritual biography of a young missionary to the Native Americans, David Brainerd. So Edwards was willing to move his very large family—eight of his children were still under the age of eighteen—to the dangerous frontier settlement to serve that cause. His Stockbridge years were among the most eventful of his life, marked especially by the outbreak, in 1754, of the French and Indian War.

In 1757 Edwards accepted a call to become the president of the College of New Jersey (Princeton). There, before moving the rest of his family from Stockbridge, he lived with his daughter Esther Burr, the widow of the Rev. Aaron Burr Sr., the late former president of the Presbyterian college. Edwards also, by the way, got to know his rambunctious two-year-old grandson, Aaron Jr. (future vice president of the United States and deadly rival of Alexander Hamilton). In 1758 in New Jersey there was a smallpox epidemic. Edwards, who respected science, advocated vaccinations, which—while even more controversial than they are today—had recently been proven to be effective; early that year, however, he died from a rare side effect.

———

As a biographer of Edwards, I find that several factors stand out for understanding him in his personal and historical context.

First, I think it is important to recognize that during most of his life Jonathan was surrounded by large families, mostly women and children. While growing up, his daily life must have been shaped very largely by his ten sisters and his highly intelligent, pious mother. In Northampton Jonathan and his wife Sarah, likewise intelligent and pious, also reared a family of eleven children, eight girls and three boys. Many of the women around him were his models for Christian piety. Due to gender biases in record keeping, we know very little about most of these women or how they influenced him.[4]

A second factor is that Edwards (d. 1758) lived in an era before the more progressive outlooks that sparked the American Revolution and other social transformations of the next century were

---

[4]Esther Edwards Burr is the one exception. See Carol F. Karlsen and Laurie Crumpacker, eds., *The Journal of Esther Edwards Burr, 1754–1757* (New Haven, CT: Yale University Press, 1986).

considerable factors in public discourse. That meant that he, his wife, Sarah, and his family took for granted some attitudes that most twenty-first-century people regard as mistaken. For instance, instead of assuming, as most of us do, that all people should be, as much as possible, afforded equal opportunities, they assumed that—as had been true throughout almost all history—societies should be arranged hierarchically and that normally men should rule. One example would be that the many gifted women in the Edwards household were, as a matter of course, not allowed collegiate education.

Most jarring to our sensibilities is the troubling fact that Edwards owned probably one or two enslaved Africans most of his career, as did many other clergy and other prominent New Englanders prior to the Revolutionary era. I have offered in *Jonathan Edwards: A Life* a detailed account of what little we know about that and his views on the subject. In summary, while Edwards was wrong to have owned enslaved Africans, he was at least ahead of his time in rejecting the underlying and more lasting racism that was used to justify mistreatment of nonwhite people. Unlike the great majority of his White contemporaries, he was explicitly antiracist, affirming that Africans, Native Americans, and Europeans were "of the same human race."[5]

---

[5]He made this observation specifically regarding Africans, and in a sermon to the Native Americans he likewise emphasized that "we are no better than you in no respect." He also affirmed that one day there would be great African and Native American theologians. In some informal notes from the 1740s he observed that while he did not believe that slavery was prohibited in the Bible, Europeans did not have the right "to disfranchise all the nations of Africa." Nonetheless, despite his antiracist views, which were progressive for his time, he indicated that the problem of African slavery was systemic in that it was sustained by the huge economic interests in the transatlantic trade system on which all the colonists were dependent. So, living at a time when antislavery sentiments were rare, he apparently believed that there was no effective way to change that system. And,

Further, within a few years of Edwards's death, both his son, Jonathan Edwards Jr., and his closest disciple, Samuel Hopkins, used his ethical teachings in their opposition to slavery.

While we can acknowledge that Edwards was wrong regarding slave owning, that fault surely does not nullify the value of his insights on many other matters. One good working principle in life is to recognize that we can learn things from people who have serious blind spots and moral failings even while we may criticize those shortcomings. And such attitudes of generosity should be especially evident regarding the blind spots of people in other eras who lived in circumstances that we only dimly understand. If we did not accept the principle that we can learn profound things from people who have serious flaws and inconsistencies, then we could not learn from anyone— excepting Jesus. And no one could learn from us.

A third factor that is particularly striking for understanding Edwards's life is that he lived much of it on the American frontier. Northampton was on the western edge of the British settlements. So Edwards's experiences were very much shaped by living in the conflicts among three powers contending for the same territories: the British, the French, and the various Native Americans whom the Europeans had displaced. Periodically during his lifetime, conflicts among these groups broke out into fierce warfare, usually as extensions of European wars. Northampton sometimes had to be fortified in fear of attack from the Native Americans. And in Stockbridge, keeping peace with the local

---

he observed, even those who did not own slaves were supporting the system by buying products produced by slaves. See George Marsden, *Jonathan Edwards: A Life* (New Haven, CT: Yale University Press, 2003), 255-58 and 385 for a fuller account and documentation regarding his views on slavery and race.

Native Americans was always a primary concern. Many of the other Native Americans were allied with the French. During the French and Indian War of the 1750s, the Edwards family was in particular danger. On occasion, cannon fire could be heard from the Edwards's home.

A fourth factor for understanding Edwards in his own time is that his British loyalties, especially during these times of periodic warfare, were heightened by the fact that he saw Great Britain as the primary defender of the Protestant cause within Christendom and particularly in North America. In the two centuries since the Reformation, Christendom had been bitterly divided between Protestants and Catholics, and that still shaped many people's political and national loyalties. Edwards's intense Protestant partisanship led him to his postmillennial interpretations of the Bible, in which the defeat of the pope as antichrist played a pivotal role.

Finally, relating to his lasting influence, there is a positive side to Edwards having lived at the time he did. Some of his most fundamental insights arise in the context of living at a turning point between two historical eras. Born in New England in 1703, he was reared in a world in which much of the premodern Puritan outlook of the previous century was still intact. Yet he was also living at the dawn of what we now see as the modern era. So at the same time that he was growing up in a little town, in a sheltered and old-fashioned Puritan environment, he was also coming of age in a colony of Great Britain just as that nation was emerging as an epicenter of the revolutionary new scientifically based thought. While still in his teens, Jonathan became thoroughly acquainted with both outlooks. As a precocious child, he early became acquainted with the Puritan theology of his father's preaching, teaching, and theological library. Then, at college in his teens, he immersed himself in the works of Isaac Newton and John Locke, who were revolutionizing the thought of his day. As his protégé, friend, and first biographer, Samuel Hopkins, put it, Edwards said concerning John Locke's volume on human understanding that he "had more satisfaction and pleasure in studying it, than the most greedy miser in gathering up handfuls of silver and gold from some newly discovered treasure."[6] He also eagerly read the witty observations and intelligence from the world of sophisticated thought in the fashionable British journal *The Spectator*, edited by Joseph Addison and Richard Steele. Such reading helped keep him current with a wide range of science, metaphysics, and philosophy, all the elements in what we now call "the Enlightenment." In his private notebooks of his late teen years, we find highly sophisticated reflections on how the modern outlooks fit with the ancient theology.

———

Creative insights involve seeing things in new ways. Often crosscultural experiences may trigger such insight—as when a visitor from a very different culture notices things that we may not see. Similarly, great thinkers who lived at dramatic turning points in their civilization have particularly profound insights as a result. Augustine is the classic case in point. Living, as he did, to witness the demise of the Roman Empire and a crisis in ancient thought as Christendom was taking shape, he offered

---

[6]Samuel Hopkins, *The Life and Character of the Late Reverend Mr. Jonathan Edwards* (S. Kneeland: Boston, 1765) as reprinted in *Jonathan Edwards: A Profile*, ed. David Levin (New York: Hill and Wang, 1969), 5-6.

profound insight on both theology and civilization. Jonathan Edwards was in a similar position. Some of his most acute inspirations arise from his being there at the dawn of a new age that still helps shape our own. Yet he also was heir to many centuries of Christian thought that had occupied some of the greatest thinkers of the Western world. Furthermore, the international Reformed or Calvinist network of theologians in which he was immersed had been—for the past century and a half—second to none in its intellectual rigor. Much of Edwards's most creative work involves reflections on how these two outlooks might illumine each other, especially in how classic Christianity might help challenge some of the most basic underlying assumptions of modernity. As we shall see, many of his best spiritual and intellectual insights remain illuminating for Christians today.

2

The CULTURE *That* FRANKLIN BUILT

ONE WAY TO gain perspective on our own time is to imagine what it would be like for a person from the past to visit our world. What would such a person think? Suppose that your job is to be a tour guide assigned to host such time-travelers from the past, to show them around, and to explain our twenty-first-century technologies, most prevalent beliefs, values, assumptions, sources of conflict, and so forth. What parts of our culture would be most difficult to explain? What might we be most proud of? What sorts of things that we take for granted would the visitor find most puzzling?

I have tried this thought experiment imagining that Jonathan Edwards himself would be the visitor. But it never goes well. There is just too much that he would find upsetting and beyond explanation. One problem would be his deep disappointment about how far the twenty-first-century reality was from his expectations. His misleading scheme for interpreting biblical prophecies had brought him to conclude that the culminating era of world history would be a wonderful thousand-year golden age, or millennium, that likely would begin around the year AD 2000. Given how far the prediction is from the reality, one can imagine spending the whole day trying to explain to Edwards why even most Christians can tolerate much of what we take for granted. As a biographer, I have found Edwards largely admirable in most respects as a person of his time and in his position. Even so, one thing that an imagined visit to the present helps bring out is that even in terms of his own times, he did not have a flexible personality. He was not good at the give-and-take of casual conversation. As in the events that led to his dismissal from Northampton, he could be unyielding even in his most controversial principles. And we are reminded once again that many of his hierarchical social and political opinions are now conspicuously out of date.

But what if, instead of Edwards, our historical guest for a tour of our civilization would be his close contemporary, Benjamin Franklin? Compared to Edwards, we might imagine, Franklin would be a delight. That would not be because Franklin was on the whole a better or more admirable person. He had some glaring faults, as we shall see. Yet as a time-traveling guest, the witty and congenial Franklin would be a pleasure compared to the more reserved, theoretically minded, and critical Edwards. Even though Franklin, too, would be shocked by some of the changes, he would take it all with wit and good humor. He would be genially inquisitive and fascinated by our accounts of how things worked and of all the changes that had taken place. Late in life, alluding to a sort of secular millennium, he wrote to the scientist Joseph Priestly, "It is impossible to imagine the height to which may be carried, in a thousand years, the power of man over matter." Franklin speculated that there might be easy air travel and such great advances in medicine as to eliminate almost all disease.[1] So Franklin would be more fascinated than surprised by the amazing developments in just over two centuries. He would also be appalled by the weapons that humans had developed that might annihilate the species, or those that had been used for genocides on almost unimaginable scales. He would be confirmed in some of his suspicions regarding the destructive qualities of selfish human nature, but he would also find much to celebrate in increased options for self-improvement. He would applaud the spread of the ideals of the self-made person, and he would appreciate most of the accelerating advances in liberty and equality, even while well recognizing that the two ideals might sometimes conflict. He would be pleased that sex had been turned from something often illicit and dangerous into a major source of recreation. Hearing that in the twenty-first century a higher percentage of Americans were churchgoers as compared to his day, he might observe that, however unbelievable some of their theologies, churches were probably good for encouraging self-improvement, acts of charity, and virtuous citizens.

He would be especially pleased to learn that upon close inspection, much of America's popular religion turned out to treat God as a sort of providential force to be called on for favors or in time of need. At the same time, he would have mixed feelings about the fusions of religion and politics. While he would think that, as a general rule, prayer that a benevolent Providence might be on the side of one's nation was a good thing, he would

---

[1]Benjamin Franklin, *The Writings of Benjamin Franklin,* ed. Albert Henry Smyth, 10 vols. (New York: Macmillan, 1905–1907), 10:10, as quoted in A. Owen Aldridge, "Enlightenment and Awakening in Edwards and Franklin," *Benjamin Franklin, Jonathan Edwards, and the Representation of American Culture,* ed. Barbara B. Oberg and Harry S. Stout (New York: Oxford University Press, 1993), 30.

be suspicious of appropriations of religion to rally people in populist political causes. He would think that governments should be run by those who were well informed and qualified, not just by popular opinion or moneyed interests. He would be very pleased and probably a bit surprised that the basics of the American Constitution were still in place and would no doubt have some thoughts as to how their applications might be improved. He would be alarmed, for instance, by how the two-party system favored power over principle and by the extent to which Americans did not demand virtue in their leaders. And he would be especially disappointed to learn that, even among many of the best educated, modernity and the Enlightenment ideal of finding rationally based moral principles had given way to postmodernity and even what has been called a "post-truth" world. He would be chagrined to learn that, instead of working together to find common ground for some sort of social consensus, so many modern people had reverted to factionalism in which right and wrong was defined mostly by whatever gave them personal freedom or benefited their own group or party.

As one who had been liberated by revolutionary advances in print technology and was a great champion of journalism and freedom of the press, Franklin would be especially fascinated by how the internet was reshaping our world. Yet he probably would also see that there are disadvantages when everyone and anyone can become a journalist who can publish or republish whatever nonsense comes into their head or onto their screen.

Whatever we might imagine as the details of a Franklin visit, one major point would come through: that our civilization today is much more like the future that Franklin imagined than it is like that which Edwards predicted and hoped for. Many of the most basic motifs of our culture today, not just in the United States but also throughout much of the world, can be seen as the pervasive overgrowth from seeds that Franklin and allies were planting in the eighteenth century: ever-increasing technology; aggressive market capitalism; celebrations of self; trying to balance liberty and equality, materialism, permissive sensuality, nationalism, and transnational consciousness—just to mention a few. Granted, we can also see the remarkable burgeoning of evangelical awakenings and other sorts of Christianity in many parts of the world. But even these often seem to be shaped in part by cultural assumptions and practices that have grown out of the more Franklinesque ideals.

So here is the question we want to get to: how can Edwards help us formulate a constructive theology in a twenty-first-century cultural setting? My central argument in these reflections is that Edwards's core vision, grounded as it is in mainstream Augustinian Christianity, has much of value to offer for renewal today. That relevance is particularly strong just because that core outlook, drawn from a particularly acute sharpening of a long tradition of Christian thought, provides striking contrasts to many of the underlying assumptions of our time and culture. So first, before reflecting on how Edwards's core vision might help us to meet the challenges of the modern civilization, I want to step back and reflect just a bit on the traits of contemporary civilization and how we got to be where we are now. So for that, it is helpful to think of Franklin as one of the founders of a modern civilization that now in its postmodern phase is often out of control.

———

Franklin's own story is fascinating. Born in Boston in January 1706, a little over two years after Edwards, Franklin was also reared in a strict Calvinist household. Young Benjamin, like young Jonathan, read whatever was available in his father's library, including a number of theological treatises. He also avidly read Cotton Mather's *Essays to Do Good*, a volume that so much impressed him that much later in life he still celebrated its moral message. Benjamin's early schooling at what became the Boston Latin School set him on a track to go to Harvard, but for reasons not altogether clear, his father instead set him to working in his candle business. It may be that by that time his religious skepticism was already becoming apparent.[2]

Despite the pervasive religious atmosphere and influence of the Calvinist clergy and allied conservative magistrates, Boston was rapidly changing in the decades when young Ben was growing up. Most strikingly, it was becoming more cosmopolitan. Boston was British America's largest city and a thriving seaport, bringing in varieties of people and outlooks. Whereas Jonathan Edwards had to rely largely on his avid reading to learn of this cosmopolitan world, Benjamin Franklin not only read everything in sight but also could participate in discussions of the latest ideas from the European world and emerging British Enlightenment.

Franklin at an early age turned from his Calvinist upbringing to a trust in self-improvement, yet it should not be assumed that he rejected religious faith as such. His Calvinist rearing left a deep impression on him. As was apparent later in life when he reflected

---

[2]Thomas S. Kidd, *Benjamin Franklin: The Religious Life of a Founding Father* (New Haven, CT: Yale University Press, 2017), 13-23, offers a nice overview. Also helpful is D. G. Hart, *Benjamin Franklin: Cultural Protestant* (New York: Oxford University Press, 2021).

on his career and philosophy in his *Autobiography*, one of the things he was inventing was a surrogate progressive and humanistic faith. This faith was not dependent on any ancient revelation but mainly on modern rationality. The test of the faith was virtue or morality. Franklin had inherited from his upbringing the Puritan heritage of serving the commonwealth and so aspired to be a person who used his intellect and resources not only to help himself but also to serve society. So he dedicated himself to all sorts of practical inventions, from lightning rods to Franklin stoves to fire companies, mutual insurance societies, and at last to helping to design a new nation. Franklin's outlook seems always to have included a substantial role for God, but he also was always something of a tinkerer or inventor as to what that meant. Like almost everyone of his time he believed that a universe with intelligent life must have been created by a higher intelligence. Franklin sometimes called himself a deist, but his sort of deism differed from the more radical kind, in which the Divine Being or Providence, like a great clockmaker, built a universe that simply ran on its own. Rather, while Franklin distanced God from everyday life, he also affirmed that Providence might sometimes benevolently intervene and that it was proper to pray for such. In general this wise and benevolent Deity helped those who helped themselves and ensured that in the long run virtue would be rewarded. Jesus was to be honored as one of the greatest of moral teachers. The more conventional Christianity of the churches and of the revivalists, including belief in a system of reward and punishment in the afterlife, was useful for promoting morality among the general populace.[3]

---

[3]Kidd, *Benjamin Franklin: Religious Life,* 4-5, 63-67, 234-35.

Franklin's religion was in many ways not only a prototype for the sophisticated eighteenth-century semi-Christian or cultural Protestant outlooks of many of America's founding fathers but also is a recognizable feature in much of the public and popular religiosity today. In the early twenty-first century, sociologist Christian Smith famously documented that the most typical religious outlook of American teenagers, even those who had been reared in traditionalist Christian churches, was "moralistic, therapeutic deism." They tended to believe that there was a benevolent, mostly distant God who wanted people to be good and who might be called on in times of sickness or crisis for help and comfort. At the same time they believed in developing one's own self-identity.[4] Franklin would be pleased.

Franklin was America's first great prophet of the self-made person. His publications, *The Way to Wealth* and his *Autobiography*, were early classics on this popular theme. The American dream is that anyone can be whatever they want to be and work hard enough for. Think how often we have heard American Olympic champions say that their success proves that "you can do anything that you want if you just try hard enough." Almost everyone who once aspired to be a brilliant athlete, musician, artist, or national leader can testify that just trying hard is not enough. But it is part of our national creed. As a church sign that I once saw put it: "THE LAST FOUR LETTERS OF AMERICAN ARE 'I CAN.'"

And even many in the contemporary Western world who do not believe in God still hold, as Franklin certainly did, to moral

---

[4]Christian Smith, *Soul Searching: The Spiritual Lives of American Teenagers* (New York: Oxford University Press, 2005).

ideals that have an identifiably Christian heritage. That is a historical trend not always recognized but most recently well documented in the historian Tom Holland's wide-ranging and engaging historical study, *Dominion*. Christ's message and example was revolutionary in the Roman Empire and then throughout Western history in celebrating the value of the poor, the weak, the outsider, and the neglected. Today, avowed secularists in many parts of the world embrace such ideals as self-evident truths.[5]

As was true in Franklin's own life, these altruistic ideals that celebrate equality often live in tension with ideals of individual freedom, success, and wealth for self-fulfillment. Prior to the Revolutionary era, Franklin was another slaveholder. And when he affirmed that "all men are created equal" in the Declaration of Independence, he, like Jefferson and other signers, was thinking mostly of the rights of White males. Franklin's exercise of his freedom for sexual gratification led to routine exploitation of women and contributed to neglect of his common-law wife and family. Jefferson's long sexual relationship with the enslaved Sally Hemings illustrates the contradiction even more tellingly. Today the contradictions between the ideals of liberty and equality are not always so stark. Yet we inevitably find a host of tensions between the two valued ideals. Maximizing freedom will increase inequalities by favoring those who are already advantaged with resources and power. In other words, as the founders recognized at least in principle, but not always in practice, liberty has to be restrained by the pursuit of justice. Yet achieving a healthy

---

[5]Tom Holland, *Dominion: How the Christian Revolution Remade the World* (New York: Basic Books, 2019).

balance between the two has always been elusive and may be more so in our day than in theirs.

One notable feature that distinguishes Franklin's time from our own is that enlightened eighteenth-century thinkers were confident that humans were on their way to finding objective moral laws that would provide standards for balancing such concerns. Since even the deists believed that the universe must have been created by an intelligent being, progressive thinkers were convinced that such objective moral laws must exist, analogous to the laws of physics discovered by Isaac Newton. These laws might be discovered by "moral philosophy" or "moral science." The first step developing such a science of morality was to establish a firm foundation in self-evident principles that all rational people ought to be able to agree on.

In the late 1600s John Locke provided a classic formulation of such ideals. Locke famously argued that we can know intuitively that humans have fundamental and "self-evident" human rights, such as rights to life, liberty, and property. In the era of Franklin and Edwards, the Scottish school of Common Sense philosophers, most notably Francis Hutcheson and Thomas Reid, were especially influential in developing this agenda. They believed that they could identify a set of self-evident foundational philosophical principles, including self-evident or "common-sense" moral principles. Then, through careful reasoning, one could build on those solid foundations a scientific system of morality. Their dream was that many long-disputed moral questions might then be settled once and for all.

Such high hopes to provide new moral foundations for civilization were not entirely far-fetched. In fact such views were so influential that one popular book on the Scottish Enlightenment is titled, with only a bit of exaggeration, *How the Scots Invented the Modern World*.[6] The immediate and also most lasting impact of those ideals came in the American Revolution. Thomas Jefferson and James Madison each got their collegiate training from Scottish teachers. Franklin offered his own informal or homemade version of such thinking. Most of the founders recognized, more than is usually acknowledged today, that human nature was seriously flawed. So the task of building a healthy and peaceful society was very difficult, since people were naturally selfish and divided into factions, ethnicities, interest groups, and parties, often with irrational loyalties.[7] Yet they nonetheless believed that such conflicting interests could at least be mitigated by checks and balances, such as those built into the American Constitution. And also essential to making the system work was to cultivate a virtuous citizenry who, despite their differences, could share in a consensus of fundamental moral principles.

Franklin and the other founders lived in an era when it was relatively easy for educated people to be optimistic about the state of the universe and about their ability to understand it without the aid of special revelation. God could be thought of as an essentially benevolent Providence who was distanced from the physical and moral workings of the universe but not entirely absent. In fact, it was almost impossible to imagine that this amazing cosmos, including intelligent beings, could have

---

[6]Arthur Herman, *How the Scots Invented the Modern World: The True Story of How Western Europe's Poorest Nation Created Our World and Everything in It* (New York: Crown Business, 2001).

[7]A very helpful recent book on this theme is Robert Tracy McKenzie, *We the Fallen People: The Founders and the Future of Democracy* (Downers Grove, IL: IVP Academic, 2021).

originated except from a Creator of higher intelligence. The "argument from design" was still compelling. One popular version was that if one were on a desert island and found a watch, one could infer with certainty that there must be a watchmaker. If so, then something far more intricate, like a whole thinking human being, must have a marvelously intelligent Creator. And such a wonderful designer, it seemed, was likely to be a benevolent being.

By a century after Franklin's time, such a view of a universe designed by something like a benevolent Providence had become antiquated in most intellectual communities. Instead, most of the best scientists and many of the best educated had been won over to the rather grim assumption that the universe was controlled solely by impersonal natural forces. The turning point was the publication in 1859 of Charles Darwin's paradigm-shifting *On the Origin of Species*. Prior to Darwin's theory of how intelligent life might emerge from random natural forces, there was no plausible explanation of how higher intelligence could emerge from mindless substances and forces. If Darwin was right, then one might still posit a God who originated the processes, but such a supposition was wholly optional. And once there was wide acceptance of something like Darwin's explanations of the origins of life based on purely naturalistic forces, then it would soon become commonplace to apply the same sorts of naturalistic explanation to things like the evolution of human morality or the evolution of religion itself.

Philosopher Charles Taylor, in his classic, *A Secular Age*, has described a more pervasive cultural phenomenon as people in the modern world came to rely primarily on naturalistic explanations for just about everything. Taylor's term for this is the "immanent frame." By that metaphor, he means that what frames or shapes the everyday outlooks of almost all modern people are considerations that are *immanent* rather than *transcendent*. Even the many people who seriously affirm beliefs in the transcendent live most of their lives so enveloped by the immanent framework of modernity that the transcendent does not practically penetrate those parts of their lives.[8] If your car breaks down or your phone has a glitch, you may pray for tranquility and patience, but you will also want to find a mechanic or technician as soon as possible. We rely so much on secular methodologies that our religious beliefs and practices often become largely supplemental. Or those who are traditionally Christian may find that they simply shift from one outlook to the other without much integrating the two. They may take care of their health, for instance, primarily by following well-planned dietary, exercise, and cleanliness practices and taking medicines. If something goes wrong, however, they also turn to God for healing. Even so, much of their hope for healing will depend largely on trusting the doctors to do the right things.

As a sort of corollary to the immanent frame, Taylor characterizes another typical result of modern disenchantment: many people take on an outlook of "exclusive humanism." He defines exclusive humanism as an outlook that operates on the practical assumption that there is "no good beyond human flourishing."[9] Like the immanent frame itself, this sort of assumption is so much part of modern education and popular culture that people take it for granted. Rather than thinking of humans'

---

[8]See James K. A. Smith, *How (Not) to Be Secular: Reading Charles Taylor* (Grand Rapids, MI: Eerdmans, 2014), 92-93, which explains immanent frame.
[9]Charles Taylor, *A Secular Age* (Cambridge, MA: Harvard University Press, 2007), 18.

relationship to God as their preeminent concern, they instinctively think first of what will promote human welfare, usually their own welfare. Even if they are religious, references to transcendent considerations may be subordinated, practically speaking, to what they see as promoting human flourishing. A good many church people today may, for instance, view God as holding just about the same views on things as can be found in the platform of their political party, whether that be conservative or progressive.

Wishing, as Franklin did, to promote individual self-fulfillment and social welfare is, of course, in many ways admirable. Franklin as a self-made person contributed, for instance, to the breakdown of hierarchy that was just beginning in the new American culture. That and the ideal of equality of opportunity have become among the most conspicuous and fruitful of American values. These have also contributed to many positive developments and reforms, such as ending slavery, bringing in principles of racial justice, creating equal opportunities for women, limiting child labor, protecting individual rights, and many other beneficial advancements.

Yet, as so often is the case in human history, the best of our ideals—just because they are evidently good in many ways—are easily turned into absolutes that transform virtues into vices. So in the modern world laudable emphases on individual rights and freedom have often turned into virtual worship of the self. Charles Taylor has described this widespread outlook as the "buffered self," by which he means that individuals often come to be buffered or insulated from any other loyalty, such as to family, community, or higher moral principles. The highest duty, as media or education often proclaim, is to be true to oneself.

David Brooks, who has been one of the most astute commentators of our times, observes that such attitudes are particularly rampant in our contemporary "moral ecology." First of these characteristic twentieth-century attitudes, says Brooks, is "the buffered self," or the belief that "the autonomous individual is the fundamental unit of society." Second is "the God within," or finding fulfillment by listening to one's own authentic voice. Third is "the privatization of meaning," or the idea that you need not look to parents or community to find a moral order, but rather you establish a moral order on your own. Fourth is "the dream of total freedom" that eats away at traditional cultural ideals such as those that come from family, ethnic heritage, faith, or nation. Fifth and finally, Brooks points out "the centrality of accomplishment" in a hyperindividualistic society. The greatest values are not measured by having deep relationships and loyalties but rather by personal achievement. Brooks notes that this list of the traits of a hyperindividualistic society is not complete and that one could add things like "consumerism, a therapeutic mindset and a preference for technology over intimacy." Whatever the details, we can all recognize such outlooks—if not in much of what we see around us, perhaps within ourselves.[10]

Almost all of these traits, we might imagine, would sound good to Benjamin Franklin if he were visiting the twenty-first century. They are, after all, ideals of which he was a principal progenitor. Yet, as David Brooks goes on to point out, they have

---

[10]David Brooks, *The Second Mountain: The Quest for the Moral Life* (New York: Random House, 2019), 10-12.

turned out to be destructive of the well-being of both individuals and society.

———

"Poor Benjamin Franklin!" you might be saying by now. Should we really be blaming *him* for all these problematic traits that have become so commonplace in our culture in the past two hundred and fifty years? That would, of course, be unfair to his memory. He could not have anticipated all the many historical forces that were far beyond his control or influence. And again we need to be reminded how often in human affairs some good principles, when taken too far, may turn into destructive idols.

Nonetheless, I am hoping that it is a helpful way of thinking about our heritage as a civilization to see Franklin as a *representative* figure who helps us understand what has been happening since the eighteenth century. Franklin, in this regard, is particularly helpful because he is such an attractive figure who so often combined interest in his own success with trying to improve the mechanisms of society around him. It would be hard to overstate how much each of us benefits every day from the traditions of technological and social innovation that Franklin did so much to promote. Yet the story of his legacy, as are so many stories in human history, is a story of the ironies of largely admirable accomplishments that bring with them some unintended consequences.

So what we can say in summary is that Franklin and the other founders of the United States promoted many ideals that we still celebrate: equal rights, individual opportunity, and "liberty and justice for all." While they realized that throughout human history such ideals had been difficult to achieve, they also were convinced that those ideals had a basis in objective moral principles built into reality by a benevolent Creator. They promoted these ideals with the hope that people of goodwill could recognize them and, despite their differences and competing self-interests, could at least work to find common ground to promote a virtuous society. Yet a gulf that separates their assumptions from the dominant outlooks in the twenty-first century is that these eighteenth-century people believed that their moral principles had a transcendent and objective basis. So one could be essentially secular and still be confident in these ideals as discovered in natural law. Today there is no longer a basis for such confidence in secular moral judgments. In a universe in which there are no knowable transcendent standards, moral principles become dependent on social location. Even though each group, as defined by ethnicities, nationalities, regions, economic interests, class, education, and gendered identities, asserts its moral principles as though they are self-evident and universal absolutes, in fact they are mostly dependent on that group's unique set of interests and assumptions. In such a setting, factionalized conflicts thrive. And in our polarized world even the best aspects of our inherited ideals typically get lost or distorted.[11]

Another force that accentuates such problems and transforms our culture and our everyday assumptions—and that Franklin could not have anticipated—is the impact of technology as it reshapes almost everything else. Franklin was, of course, one of

---

[11]For an account of the demise of these enlightenment views in the mid-twentieth century, see George Marsden, *The Twilight of the American Enlightenment* (New York: Basic Books, 2014).

the greatest early champions of improving civilization through technology. And, as we have observed, he would be extremely pleased by many of its amazing contemporary applications, even if he would be alarmed by its destructive potential. Yet our pervasive dependence on technologies has a deeper impact in shaping our lives and sensibilities than we may realize.

Already in the mid-twentieth century the Christian sociologist Jacques Ellul presented a compelling portrait of "the technological society" that had emerged by that time. The overriding demand in a technological society, he observed, is to find the most rational and efficient way to get things done. These technological habits of thinking are a major force in diminishing our sense of anything transcendent. As technologies multiply and we gain increasing control over our circumstances, the world has been increasingly "disenchanted," or emptied of mystery and deeper meaning. And the impact of technology goes well beyond just being able to use machines and other inventions, such as medicine, as revolutionary and often helpful as those innovations are. The technological principle of finding the most rational and efficient way to get things done often seems almost to take on, in effect, a will of its own when adopted by major organizations, such as industries, businesses, and governments. Totalitarian governments have been among the most alarming expression of such modern impulses to efficiently organize everything. But even in "free" societies the wills of individuals are often subordinated to the demands of efficient organization. Our society often takes for granted that efficiency is simply a good thing. Yet think, for instance, of the countless people who have been forced to engage in mind-numbing, regimented manufacturing labor in order to make a living. Our ancestors may have had to engage in backbreaking agricultural labor and to be subject to the whims of nature, but their relationship to their work could also be meaningful. And as Wendell Berry reminds us in his novels, people lived and worked in tightly knit families and communities. In modern times, people often move away from their families and from the communities in which they were reared. The demands of efficient manufacturing or marketing take on a seeming blind will of their own that humans can only partially control. We take almost for granted, for instance, that a corporation may move its employees from city to city with no concern for the values of home, community, church congregation, or other personal considerations.[12]

Later in the twentieth century, Christopher Lasch described one result of such forces in countries such as the United States as a "culture of narcissism." People whose highest value is to be self-fulfilled look to experts to guide them in almost every aspect of their lives. Yet they are plagued by anxiety in a search not so much for meaning as to be successful and admired. As sociologist Robert Bellah similarly observed in his classic study of that same era, *Habits of the Heart*, Americans typically depended on the manager and the therapist to guide their lives. Rather than searching for meaning, they were more often looking for guidance to establish a viable "lifestyle."[13]

In the twenty-first century we all have become aware of how such trends have been accelerated by the pervasiveness of the electronic media. More than ever we see the power of

---

[12]Jacques Ellul, *The Technological Society* (New York: Knopf, 1964).

[13]Christopher Lasch, *The Culture of Narcissism* (New York: Warner, 1979). Robert Bellah et al., *Habits of the Heart* (Berkeley: University of California Press, 1985).

technology in shaping what we think, how we think, and how we relate to others. One notable impact is that such media accentuate hyperindividualism as each of us can shape whatever we see each day to suit our personal tastes. At the same time these personal choices often reinforce tribalism, exclusive identities, or superficial communities. In the twentieth century, propaganda machines could establish monopolies on the media of a totalitarian state. Today, almost anyone can become a propagandist or buy into one of countless competing propagandist claims. Ironically, while we have incredibly more information in our phones at our fingertips than did even the very best-informed persons only a generation ago, false information seems to flourish as never before. Tribalism plus electronic media invites instant conflict and often-viral spread of unfounded claims. In this "post-truth" era, electronic media encourage people to find immediate support for believing just about anything or anyone they want to believe. Rather than bringing us together, the increase in knowledge seems to be resulting in a new Tower of Babel. Chaos ensues.

One thing to underscore—once again—about these ever-increasing technological forces is how they can reinforce the tendencies of modern people to be cut off from a sense of the transcendent. When Charles Taylor talked about modern people becoming insulated from the transcendent, he was citing trends that were already apparent by the mid-nineteenth century. Since then, modern technologies have vastly changed our lives, and in the twenty-first century the dominating influences of technologies have been accelerating at ever-increasing rates.

It should go without saying that Jonathan Edwards does not provide the complete answers to all these twenty-first-century challenges. Yet his fundamental view of reality, drawn for the long history of Christian theology, offers a radical starting point for thinking about what it should mean to follow Christ in our own disruptive contemporary era. Living (as he did) as a contemporary of Franklin, just when some of the most basic outlooks that would reshape the modern world were emerging, he offered some truly striking alternatives.

3

The DYNAMIC
BEAUTY *of* GOD

EDWARDS'S GREATEST INSIGHTS arose in the context of living at the intersection of two remarkably attractive worlds, the formidable New England Puritan heritage and the cosmopolitan, British, enlightened culture of the eighteenth century. His personal encounter with these two impressive cultures was a deeply existential one for Edwards. His father, Timothy Edwards, was a strict and impressive New England pastor. Timothy preached without compromise the inherited Reformed doctrine of the sovereignty of God in all things. One of the tendencies of that Calvinist heritage was that, when regarding any of the classic paradoxes of understanding the relationship of God's rule to the actions of his creation and creatures, they would give as much credit to God as was possible. They were saying, in effect—though of course they would not have put it quite this way—"if we err in explaining these paradoxes, it should be on the side of giving too much credit to God rather than too much credit to humans." So, for instance, such Reformed preachers and teachers constantly emphasized the sovereignty of God in eternally ordering all things, even while they acknowledged that God used second causes, such as the laws of physics, that could be understood as God's way of governing the operations of the material world. Or, while strict Calvinists stressed that ultimately our wills are subject to God's eternal degrees, and particularly our ability to properly love God depends entirely on God's saving grace, they also emphasized that humans willed meaningful choices for which God held them wholly responsible.

That paradox of God's determinism and our choice, particularly when it applied to one's ability to respond to God's grace, stood at the existential center of the sometimes agonizing and sometimes exhilarating Puritan experience. Pastors such as Timothy Edwards preached repeatedly on the necessity of conversion, or a true change of heart. Yet the Catch-22 was that regeneration or rebirth was not something you could accomplish on your own. It had to be a matter of your own free willing, but that became possible only through the light of God's grace that changed your heart from self-love to loving God. Even though there was no way simply to will such a change on one's own, Puritans such as Timothy Edwards constantly urged the unconverted to prepare the groundwork for salvation by performing all their Christian duties to the best of their ability. Yet good works, however obligatory, could never earn salvation. Timothy Edwards faithfully preached these doctrines, seeking above all that God might use his preaching, teaching, prayers, and urgings to employ the means of grace to bring changes of heart to his parishioners. Such preaching had its effects, as Timothy oversaw several unusual times of awakenings during his years as pastor in East Windsor. And we can be sure that he sought nothing more than the conversion of his eleven children—and no one more than his precocious only son.

Jonathan struggled with this pressure from an early age. As a young child, he later recalled, he more or less played at being super-pious. For instance, he built a hideout where he could go for secret prayers. But as a teenager he began to have serious doubts. Such questioning was certainly accentuated by his collegiate studies and his encounters not only with Locke and Newton but also with others of sophisticated British thought who kept him current with a world that had moved beyond sectarian religion. While such exposure to the modern world helped raise doubts, Jonathan continued to wrestle with the question of whether he had ever been truly converted. Thanks to his father, he was thoroughly versed in the Puritan literature of conversion. Puritans did not expect conversion to be simply a sudden moment of joy bells ringing in your heart. Rather they saw it as most typically a gradual process. And like early modern scientists, they developed a sophisticated science of the usual steps of conversion that would help them tell the difference between true converts and the hypocrites or the self-deluded. Jonathan knew that he did not measure up by such standards. And that was a terrifying thing, given that one's eternal destiny— heaven or hell—was at stake. Furthermore, such anxieties were especially strong in an era when death at an early age was not at all unusual. Jonathan himself recorded that when still a teenager in his last year at college, he experienced a serious fever that "brought me near the grave and shook me over the pit of Hell."[1]

---

[1] Jonathan Edwards, "Personal Narrative" (c. 1740), in *Letters and Personal Writings*, ed. George S. Claghorn, vol. 16 in *The Works of Jonathan Edwards* (New Haven, CT: Yale University Press, 1998), 790-804. The twenty-six-volume print edition

In addition to his doubts about himself were his questions regarding Calvinist teachings. "From my childhood up," he wrote in his later narrative of his spiritual journey, "my mind had been wont to be full of objections against the doctrine of God's sovereignty, in choosing whom he would to eternal life, and rejecting whom he pleased, leaving them eternally to perish, and be everlastingly tormented in hell. It used to appear like a horrible doctrine to me."[2]

The eighteenth-century British intellectual world in which Jonathan was immersed was beginning increasingly to value innate human rights and so to question arbitrary authority. So, for instance, John Locke provided a rationale for the British revolution of 1688 that had replaced the Catholic King James II with Protestant rulers William and Mary. Rather than appealing just to religious considerations, Locke appealed to universal and self-evident "rights of man." Locke argued that if we imagined civilization when it first emerged from a state of nature, we could surmise that the very reason why governments were established was to protect certain basic human rights, such as the rights to life, liberty, and property. For someone like the young Edwards, who surely approved of the Glorious Revolution that brought a Protestant to the English throne in 1688, such reflections could have disturbing theological implications. If it was self-evidently wrong for human rulers to treat their subjects in arbitrary ways, would we not expect God to abide by at least as

---

of the works were published with various editors between 1957 and 2006. They will be cited hereafter in this chapter as *WJE* with volume number and page. All the writings of Edwards are also readily available and searchable at The Works of Jonathan Edwards Online, http://edwards.yale.edu/archive, from the Jonathan Edwards Center at Yale University.

[2]Edwards, "Personal Narrative," 791-92.

high a standard? So how could one believe that a wholly sovereign God would eternally decree that some people would be condemned to hell while others would be granted the gift of eternal bliss in heaven?

Jonathan came to resolve this troubling moral issue not through some sort of clever moral calculus but rather by somehow coming to see God's sovereignty in a much broader light. He did not equate this new insight or sensibility—or what we might call a "paradigm shift"—exactly with his conversion experience. Rather, as he later recounted, he rather abruptly found that "I . . . had quite another kind of sense of God's sovereignty, than I had [earlier]. I have often since, not only had a conviction, but a *delightful* conviction." And he then goes on to speak of his experiences of an "inward, sweet delight in God and divine things."[3]

To understand how Jonathan came to this new sensibility, recall that he had earlier come to be deeply impressed by the new science, the immensity of the Copernican universe, and the amazing Newtonian understanding that everything was always moving, changing, in interconnected relationships, governed by comprehensive laws. Like the young Franklin, young Edwards was fascinated by natural science. His earliest work, which he had hoped to publish, was on the behavior of flying spiders. By later in his teens he was working on some very sophisticated metaphysical philosophical reflections about the fundamental nature of the universe. The most revealing emphasis of these was

---

[3]Edwards, "Personal Narrative," 792-93.

that, like some of the other greatest philosophers of the era (the philosopher Bishop George Berkeley is the closest counterpart), he concluded that the physical universe exists most meaningfully as it is perceived through the minds of intelligent beings. Edwards pointed out, for instance, that the new optics taught that the color green does not exist in leaves themselves. Rather the leaves absorb the rays that make the *other* colors and reflect only those that our eyes perceive as green. So the color green would not exist if there were no minds to perceive it. Edwards offers some similar examples to make the point that the reality of the universe depends in some essential sense on the minds that perceive it.[4] Material things, after all, have a very fleeting existence, since the arrangements of atoms that make them up are constantly in flux. Minds, however, can provide the continuity that constitutes a lasting identity. And when the material thing is gone, the idea of it will persist in the mind.

Edwards uses this illustration:

> The lucid color or brightness of the moon, as we look steadfastly upon it, seems to be a permanent thing, as though it were perfectly the same brightness continued. But indeed it is an effect produced every moment. It ceases, and is renewed, in each successive point of time; and so becomes altogether a new effect at each instant: and no one

---

[4]Jonathan Edwards, "Of Being" (1721), in *A Jonathan Edwards Reader*, ed. John E. Smith, Harry S. Stout, and Kenneth P. Minkema (New Haven, CT: Yale University Press, 1995), 17. Edwards recognizes that this way of thinking, which he was outlining in a private notebook, is obscure and can be misleading. He states, "When we say that the world, that is the material universe, exists nowhere but in the mind, we have got to such a degree of abstractness that we must be exceedingly careful that we do not confound and lose ourselves by misapprehension." Edwards, "The Mind" (1723), in *Reader*, 29.

thing that belongs to it is numerically the same that existed
in the preceding moment. The rays of the sun, impressed
on that body, and reflected from it, which cause the effect,
are none of them the same: the impression, made in each
moment on our sensory, is by the stroke of new rays: and
the sensation, excited by the stroke, is a new effect, an
effect of a new impulse.

So, he goes on, the moon has no more numerical continuity
than does the wind from moment to moment, yet our minds
constitute the moon as one thing.[5]

These speculations seem abstract and impractical in themselves, yet when combined with a Christian account of the
universe, they helped bring young Edwards to a dramatic paradigm shift. If the existence of the universe depends in some
essential way on the minds that perceive it, then it exists most
fully as it is perceived by the mind of God, its Creator and
Sustainer. Jonathan made a point of saying that our recognition that the highest form of reality is as it exists in minds
does not prevent us from also thinking about the material
things in the everyday way of common sense and in natural
science as having real existence external to us.[6] But even when
studying the physical world in that common-sense way, we
should also be aware that we are studying things that depend
on God's creation and ongoing sustenance and have their most
essential existence as perceived in the mind of God. This
observation was consistent with the standard Christian doctrines of multiple levels of causation or of the *concursus* of

---

[5]Jonathan Edwards, *Original Sin*, ed. Clyde A. Holbrook, *WJE* 3:403n.
[6]Edwards, "The Mind" (1723), in *Reader*, 29.

God's creative and providential actions in sustaining the universe yet doing so through natural processes. Still, if we shift our *primary* perspective from regarding the material universe as the most real thing to seeing everything as *most essentially* expressions of the mind of God, then we can see that starting with that perspective involves a stunning shift in perspective with implications that can lead us to perceive everything in a new light.

———

That new light, as Edwards saw it, was stunning because it was an intensely and uniquely Christian light. It was not just an abstract new philosophical perspective asserting, as had the Greek philosophers, that ideas had more permanent existence than did transitory material things. In the Christian view, the Creator God is essentially personal. In fact the triune God is revealed, remarkably, as three persons, even if of a single essence. Furthermore the most fundamental quality of these three persons is that they are loving. So the universe is not simply the product of the divine being, it is the expression of an essentially loving and always active God.

Novelist Marilynne Robinson testifies to the attractiveness of this approach as a fresh way of seeing in the contemporary world. Robinson emphasizes the centrality in her own outlook of appreciating beauty and credits Edwards with helping her to reorient her thinking. Mentioning the passage cited above concerning the continuity of the moon, she says that encountering it as a college student "gave me a new model of reality." She goes on:

Edwards rescued me out of the deprivations of what we've called "modern thought," and I have been reading him in that light ever since. He is a wonderful thinker. He's called the greatest philosopher born on the North American continent, and he is. He deserves his reputation.[7]

Edwards's outlook that the universe is most essentially an ongoing expression of a loving God offered a dramatically radical alternative to the emerging sophisticated perspective on the universe shared by Franklin and others in the era following the work of Isaac Newton. In Franklin's universe, reality is first of all about the material universe governed by natural laws that were subject to scientific observation, at least in principle. A creator was necessary to explain the existence of this vast universe, but that was a secondary consideration, and opinions varied widely as to how much that creator might also intervene providentially. In any case, the universe was understood as most essentially existing as a vast set of constantly moving and interacting material entities. So, even though it contained creatures with minds, it was understood primarily through studying the interactions of mindless material objects and forces.

In striking contrast is the magnificent Christian view of the universe. Rather than being most essentially the product of vast interacting material forces, it is a *personal* expression of the exploding or overflowing love of the loving triune God. Scientists today speculate about the "Big Bang" that seems necessary to explain the origins of the universe. If we adopt the

---

[7]Marilynne Robinson and Cherie Harder, "Story, Culture, and the Common Good: Marilynne Robinson in Conversation with Cherie Harder," *Breaking Ground: Charting Our Future in a Pandemic Year*, ed. Anne Snyder and Susannah Black (Walden, NY: Plough Publishing House, 2022), 148.

Edwardsean paradigm shift, we can think about those origins as at their deepest level the Big Bang of God's love. Everything is indeed related to everything else, as in the post-Newtonian universe, but in a universe that is the expression of overflowing love, the most essential relationships, by far, are personal. Everything is related to everything else because everything is related to the loving triune God. After all, the central starting point in the Christian account of things is that God is one being in three *persons*: Father, Son, and Holy Spirit. These three persons, perfect in love to each other, have created the universe to share that love with other beings capable of voluntarily loving. So everything is either related to God harmoniously as a response to or expression of proper love, or it is an expression of disharmony reflecting the rejection of true love in favor of lesser loves. It is persons, then, not impersonal material forces, who are at the center of reality. And seemingly impersonal material forces take on their significance as they relate to persons. Material things are expressions of the *language* of God's love. But in a fallen universe, where some persons have rebelled against God's love, that loving language is often obscured.

There is enough of a parallel that it can be illuminating to call Edwards the "Isaac Newton of theology," yet we should also recognize an important difference. Newton developed a radically new paradigm to explain the physical mechanics of the vast post-Copernican universe. Edwards was one of the first, perhaps the first, to apply the older Augustinian paradigm to this same vast universe. While Newton posited that dynamic but *impersonal* forces explained the physical interactions throughout the universe, Edwards, while accepting these, explained the most essential underlying dynamics as nonetheless *personal* interactions—attractions and repulsions. As in Augustine, the core force is intertrinitarian love, and those divine persons are constantly interacting with the loves of other persons in the universe. For Newton himself and for many post-Newtonian theists, the deity might be invoked as the supernatural force that we need to explain what physical forces cannot explain—as what later came to be called "the God of the gaps." For Edwards, the dynamics of the physical universe were to be understood and admired *most essentially* as beautiful expressions of the love of their Creator and Sustainer. And not just in the gaps, but *everywhere*.

———

The dynamic beauty of love, then, is at the center of reality. It is neither just the beauty of amazing physical phenomena that scientists talk about nor the older Platonic ideal of changeless perfections. Rather it is the beauty of ongoing loves. It is the beauty of loving or harmonious personal relationships. *Harmonious* calls up musical analogies. Unloving relationships are disharmonious and mar the beauty of the grand harmonies that God wants creatures to join in. Individuals become preoccupied with their own interests or group; nations and differing peoples try to create tunes of their own. These may have immediate appeal for those in the group, but they always fail and only offer limited lesser loves. They are like individuals whistling their own catchy melodies or perhaps like various little bands each loudly playing their own national anthems and fight songs and drowning out the harmonies of love that are in fact at the center of reality.

C. S. Lewis provides what has become one of the best-known versions of this theme of harmony at the heart of reality in The Chronicles of Narnia. Drawing on the classical and Christian traditions of the music of the spheres, the lion Aslan creates Narnia by singing a song. Aslan is the Christ figure, so Lewis is drawing on John 1:1 that "in the beginning was the Word" and that Word is Christ, who is most fully revealed to us in his sacrificial love on the cross. For Edwards, likewise, the beautiful harmonies that bring reality into being are essentially emanations of a loving person. That Word of love is the very creative heart of the universe. Yet because of our sin, which focuses us on ourselves and on our own lesser circles of loves, we do not hear those harmonies. Lewis makes the same point in *The Magician's Nephew*, the story of the creation of Narnia. When Aslan is singing Narnia into being, the magician, Uncle Andrew, who is actually a thoroughly modern "scientific" man, does not hear the song. All he hears is a lion's roar. As he remarks, "Who ever heard of a lion singing?"[8]

Edwards, who did perceive the harmonies of Christ's love permeating reality, particularly delighted in singing as a response to encountering such beauty. Music, he said, is "the best most perfect way that we have of expressing a sweet concord of mind."[9] Music likely played an important role in his

---

[8]C. S. Lewis, *The Magician's Nephew* (1955; repr., Hong Kong: Enrich Spot, Ltd., 2016), 98.

[9]Jonathan Edwards, Miscellany 188, in *Miscellanies, a–500*, ed. Thomas A. Schafer, *WJE* 13:331. Cited in Belden C. Lane, *Ravished by Beauty: The Surprising Legacy of Reformed Spirituality* (New York: Oxford University Press, 2011), 170. Edwards also observed that in heaven "there would be infinitely more proportionate,

relationship with Sarah. Jonathan also worked hard to improve the singing of his congregation, encouraging the use of four-part harmonies. And during the first wonderful Northampton awakening that occurred in 1734 and 1735, he noted the excellence of the townspeople's singing as one of the expressions of their new attitudes. He also remarked that in his personal religious devotions "it always seemed natural to me to sing, or chant forth my meditation."[10]

Edwards's New England was behind much of the rest of eighteenth-century Christendom in musical expression. The Puritans, trying to confine themselves to practices of the New Testament church, did not allow musical instruments in the church. Also, they only sang biblical psalms. Congregational singing was often off-key, improvised, and awful. Edwards helped improve the singing and defended the use of hymns, such as those of Isaac Watts, as well as psalms. One might wonder what the relation of music to awakening might have been had Edwards been in a different Protestant tradition. For instance, J. S. Bach, who expressly celebrated the Creator and Redeemer with magnificent harmonies, first offered his *Christmas Oratorio* for his Lutheran church in Leipzig in the Christmas season of 1734, exactly the same time that the amazing awakening was building in Edwards's distant parish. In New England, not only was musical development at a limited stage, but Puritans did not celebrate Christmas. Still, at the Northampton church, the unaccompanied four-part a cappella

---

harmonious and delightful" musical possibilities than in "our gross air," and that mutual delight in unlimited musical expressions would be one thing bringing God's people lovingly together (Miscellany 188).

[10]Edwards, "Personal Narrative," in *Letters, WJE* 16:794.

singing, often expressing their newly found or deepening commitments, was truly exhilarating.[11]

Belden C. Lane, in his insightful exposition of the centrality of beauty in Edwards's experiences and thought, suggests that Edwards would have been delighted by the image suggested by Hans Urs von Balthasar in his book *Truth Is Symphonic*. Balthasar proposes that we think of our universe like a symphony warming up. We are at the moment when individual musicians are on stage each practicing on their own, so that what we hear is cacophony, though perhaps with riffs of beauty occasionally shining through. But then someone sounds the A note, and all are ready to come together. "Each member of the orchestra, with eyes fixed on the Maestro, contributes to what becomes a grand celebration of the beauty and glory of God." Lane thinks Edwards would have relished such an image because he viewed creation as though it were a vast symphonic work. "Metaphors of the world as a theater of God's glory, a school of desire, or a vast orchestral work suggest the manner in which he rooted his theology in the concept of beauty." Even in the midst of present cacophony he could discover and delight in the harmonies that point toward the heavenly consummation, when all eyes will be fixed on the Creator and Redeemer.[12]

———

That brings us to a profound implication of recognizing the beauty of perfect love being constantly communicated at the

---

[11]One can find examples today of such exhilarating singing in some Churches of Christ and related churches in the Restorationist tradition who still do not use musical instruments in church worship.

[12]Lane, *Ravished*, 170-71.

heart of reality: the harmonies of perfect love imply the possibility of the disharmonies of hatred or enmity. As the nineteenth-century New England theologian Horace Bushnell remarked, "Our God is not a summer God only, but a winter God," and "whatever else may be true, God created venom."[13] We can often hear the creation sing, but the creation also groans. It contains immense destructive powers and seemingly pointless suffering. We are all liable to that suffering at any moment. The creation moans as the disharmonies cry out to be made right.

Whatever the explanations of why a perfectly loving God would permit evil, for Christians the only answer that makes the other considerations adequate is that God participates in our suffering. In the incarnation and Christ's suffering on the cross, God takes on intense, real suffering, not only excruciating agonies but also the maddening suffering of injustice. And Christ's suffering is an expression of the highest love imaginable, the suffering of the innocent on behalf of the guilty. So when we see the disharmonies of creation around us—the suffering of others—and when we experience suffering ourselves, these should point us to see suffering love on the cross as the center of reality. This reality may be overwhelmingly evil in the short run, but it also comes with the higher promise of redemption and triumph over that evil. C. S. Lewis, who in *The Problem of Pain* explores many explanations of why God permits evil, relies ultimately on this central Christian defense of God's goodness. His epigraph for that book is a quotation from George MacDonald: "The Son of God suffered unto the death, not that men might not

---

[13]Horace Bushnell, *Nature and the Supernatural* (New York: Scribners, 1871), 74. Quoted in Lane, *Ravished*, 231.

suffer, but that their sufferings might be like His."[14] In Narnia, the lion Aslan, who is ready to suffer unto the death for others, is the center of reality and the very cause of its being.

Edwards likewise viewed Christ's sacrificial love as not only at the center of created reality but as life's greatest solace in the face of evil and suffering. He expresses such consolations with passion and unusual eloquence in a lengthy letter of condolence to a Lady Pepperhill, who had recently lost her only son. "All the perfections of the Deity," he assures her, "have their brightest manifestation in the work of redemption, vastly more than in the work of creation. And our seeing in the bright light the meaning of that redemptive love is our ultimate consolation." Though he wrote the letter as prose, it is as close to poetic as he ever got. And it is an impassioned tribute to Christ's love:

> He suffered, that we might be delivered. His soul was exceedingly sorrowful even unto death, to take away the sting of sorrow and that we might have everlasting consolation. He was oppressed and afflicted, that we might be supported. He was overwhelmed in the darkness of death and hell, that we might have the light of life. He was cast into the furnace of God's wrath, that we might swim in the rivers of pleasure. His heart was overwhelmed in a flood of sorrow and anguish, that our hearts might be filled and overwhelmed with a flood of eternal joy.[15]

In his own meditations, Edwards often contemplated the beauties of creation as they pointed to the beauty of the Creator,

---

[14]C. S. Lewis, *The Problem of Pain*, The Complete C. S. Lewis Signature Classics (New York: HarperOne, 2002), iii.
[15]Edwards to Lady Mary Pepperell, 1751, in *Letters*, *WJE* 16:418.

most fully manifest in Christ's sacrificial love. The created beauties that we can see around us are not just impersonal wonders of nature, but rather they are personal expressions of their Creator. Edwards remarks that we experience something similar when we encounter the beauty of another person. Likely thinking of his admiration for Sarah, he wrote in an early devotional reflection:

When we see beautiful airs of look and gesture, we naturally think the mind that resides within is beautiful. We have all the same, and more, reason to conclude the spiritual beauty of Christ from the beauty of the world, for all the beauties of the universe do as immediately result from the efficiency of Christ, as a cast of an eye or a smile of the countenance depends on the efficiency of the human soul.[16]

In a similar reflection, he observes that "when we love the person for the airs of voice, countenance, and gesture," we see in those "excellencies of mind." He then goes on, rhapsodizing:

So that when we are delighted with flowery meadows and gentle breezes of wind, we may consider that we only see the emanations of the sweet benevolence of Jesus Christ; when we behold the fragrant rose and lily, we see his love and purity. So the green trees and fields, and singing of birds, are the emanations of his infinite joy and benignity; the easiness and naturalness of trees and vines [are] shadows of his infinite beauty and loveliness; the crystal rivers and murmuring streams have the footsteps of his sweet grace and bounty.

---

[16]Edwards, Miscellany 185, in *Miscellanies a–500*, *WJE* 13:330.

When we behold the light and brightness of the sun, the golden edges of an evening cloud, or the beauteous bow, we behold the adumbrations of his glory and goodness; and the blue skies, of his mildness and gentleness. There are also many things wherein we may behold his awful majesty: in the sun in his strength, in comets, in thunder, in the towering thunder clouds, in ragged rocks and the brows of mountains. That beauteous light with which the world is filled in a clear day is a lively shadow of his spotless holiness and happiness, and delight in communicating himself.[17]

On beautiful days Edwards loved to go out riding into the meadows and woods on horseback, relishing the glimpses of the love of Christ communicated in creation. He in fact kept notebooks on "Images of Divine Things," noting "types" of Christ and of biblical doctrines of salvation in what he saw. Those "types" included the ugly or dark sides of creation that he saw as being there to point us to the light. So the ravens that feed on dead animals are "remarkable types of devils who with delight prey upon the souls of the dead." Or dead rotten carcasses are "the lively image of a wicked man that is spiritually and exceeding filthy and abominable."[18] The snakes that charm birds and squirrels were biblical images for the devil enticing sinners. They draw their victims toward their favorite lusts until Satan finally makes prey of them. Even so, such evil in creation is to show us that "the way in which poor souls are delivered from the snare of the devil is by Christ's coming and bruising the serpent's head."[19]

---

[17]Edwards, Miscellany 108, in *Miscellanies a–500, WJE* 13:280.
[18]Edwards, "Images of Divine Things, 61," in *Reader*, 17.
[19]Edwards, "Images of Divine Things, 63," in *Reader*, 18.

Edwards sees what we call nature as having a most essential personal dimension because he takes seriously the biblical image that the created world speaks the language of God. "The heavens declare the glory of God," and "day unto day uttereth speech," as Psalm 19 puts it. God's language in nature is sometimes difficult to read, since creation has been corrupted as a result of the fall. But since the language of creation speaks of redemption, it is a message to be read in the context of evil and corruption. The beauty of the love revealed in redemption is highlighted amid the strife and violence of competing lesser loves in fallen creation. Christ, *the Word*, was "in the beginning" and "without him was not any thing made" (John 1:1-3). And at the end of time, Christ the Lamb and Redeemer declares, "I make all things new." That renewal comes with the promise that "God shall wipe away all tears from their eyes; and there shall be no more death, neither sorrow, nor crying, neither shall there be any more pain: for the former things are passed away" (Revelation 21:5, 4). So in this biblically refracted view of reality, we can appreciate how Edwards saw the stunning beauty even in fallen nature as language to remind us of the beauty of the redemptive work of Christ.

A most illuminating point to notice here is that if we view reality through the prism of Scripture, that will bring out the beauty of God's love in creation and redemption—and that, in turn, should modify our sensibilities about everything else. We can be reminded once again that in the post-Newtonian world, most modern people—like the deists of Edwards's time—have *distanced* God from creation. Like Franklin or Jefferson, they believed in a God, but their deity worked essentially through laws of nature.

And still today, even Christians are acculturated to perceive reality as made up of essentially impersonal or material forces. And, as Charles Taylor suggests when speaking of an immanent frame, the materialist assumptions of our civilization tend to create a virtual wall that blocks our recognition of transcendence. We can, if we make a point of it, look beyond the wall as we seek God and transcendence. And we may ask God occasionally—or even frequently—to come down and intervene. We still are conditioned, though, in our modern civilization, to think of such interventions as exceptions to the rule that things are determined by natural forces. We learn from an early age to think of the universe as most essentially material and therefore run by the laws known by natural science. The dominant scientific view of the past 150 years is that we have an essentially dead universe in which living things sometimes happen to pop up. Technology vastly increases the domain of that impersonal universe and its influence shaping our lives. Today even toddlers learn that electronic devices are the quickest way to make entertaining things happen. And thereafter throughout our lives, devices and techniques shape how we earn livings, how we spend our money, how we value other people, how we communicate, how we are entertained, and often how we worship.

Edwards offers an alternative sensibility to the modern distancing of God from the creation. If creation is part of the language of God, then God is intimately related to all reality. Without God's creative power sustaining the universe, things would cease to exist. So creation is not just something that happened long ago but is also an ongoing process. Yet that divine sustaining of all reality is not just an impersonal power. Rather, as Christ was the Word at the beginning of creation, so all creation continues to point toward the redemptive love of God in Christ. Hence when we view nature, we do not see it properly unless we first see it in its primary relationship, its relationship to God and God's love. So the most essential underlying dimension of reality is God's love. That means that, instead of seeing the universe as primarily a physical thing to which persons are added, we should see it as *first of all* a personal expression that happens to include things that have physical dimensions. Furthermore, that personal expression has love at its center. However much that may be obscured by evil and groaning, love is the light that shines at its brightest through the darkness. So for created persons such as we are, the primary dynamic at the heart of our experience of reality is shaped by how we are responding to that personal love. Are we open to being embraced by that love? Or do we reject it because our deeper loves are for self and for other created things?

Taking delight in the beauty of God's creation as a personal expression of God's language should also be an incentive for taking care of our environment. Belden C. Lane develops this theme not only as it relates to Edwards but to the entire Reformed tradition of which Edwards is a part.[20] In brief, if we recognize this loving personal dimension of the created order, then we should want to protect and care for it as an expression of God's love. One of the ways in which the created world is fallen, especially in recent centuries, is through humans using it

---

[20]Lane, *Ravished*, esp. 211-36.

purely for selfish purposes, convenience, and profits. Now in the twenty-first century we have some powerful practical incentives to take better care of the environment, just for our survival and welfare. Yet if our highest love is for the Creator, who speaks in the creation, that will add reasons to protect the earth and its beauty that go beyond just weighing the practical benefits and dangers. And in that critical task of weighing benefits and dangers, those who love the Creator and Christ, the Word since the beginning of creation, will order their lesser loves accordingly. That should mean that in assessing environmental policy they will be taking into account not only the practical costs and benefits for their own nation or group but also how the policies might protect and benefit peoples of the whole world, especially the poor and most vulnerable.

God's being intimately involved in creation and speaking through it does not mean, of course, that nature is in any sense identical with God. Our language, even though it is a vital expression of ourselves, is not identical with us. The same goes for a work of art that we create, even while its beauty may be speaking from the deepest part of our soul. So we can see a personal dimension in created and providentially sustained reality that surrounds us. And with the aid of the prism of Scripture we can see that these are creative expressions of the loving persons of the Trinity, pointing us particularly to the redemptive work of Christ. Yet as in our own artwork, there is much in it not identical with the Creator. That is especially so in a created universe where persons are the highest form of being. Not everything personal that we might perceive in it is a direct expression of God. In this immense universe, created persons have the ability to rebel against the Creator, however mysterious it might seem that God would permit evil.

One very imperfect but in some ways helpful analogy is to think of the universe as being like an immense computer program that, while being made, sustained, and ultimately determined by its all-knowing and all-powerful Creator, yet includes persons who are capable of choosing, loving, rebelling, reproducing, etc. Such an analogy can be helpful for trying to think how determinism and freedom for meaningful choice might be compatible. Also, if the program had lots of randomness built in, it would be both ultimately determined but effectively unpredictable. Within that framework, creatures capable of meaningful love for the Creator would also be capable of loving other things more. In other words, they would be capable of turning against the prescriptive will of a perfect and loving Creator even while the Creator had ultimately designed the universe that made such rebellion possible.

Whether or not one finds this Creator/programmer analogy helpful, the Christian view of things is that the sovereign and loving Creator God has permitted evil to thrive for a time in our universe. Or, as Edwards emphasized in biblical terms, Satan is still on the loose, and there is much that needs to be recognized as evil.

Think of the sensibility concerning the personal reality of evil C. S. Lewis attempts to recapture in *The Screwtape Letters*. That classic was written near the outset of World War II, when human evil seemed to be reaching one of its all-time crescendos. Yet cultural analysts, historians, and other observers had no adequate explanations for how humans, especially those in the "most advanced civilizations," could be so evil. And they had no solutions beyond countering horrible brute force with horrible brute force. Richard F. Lovelace, in his classic *Dynamics of Spiritual Life*, taking into account the reality of spiritual forces for good or for evil, described our efforts to observe and analyze human history as being "as confusing as a football game in which half the players are invisible."[21] By the 1940s modern sensibilities had already moved so far from recognizing Satan as a force that humor was the only way Lewis could effectively make his point. In the twenty-first century it remains just as difficult, even for many Christians, to take Satan's agency seriously. Yet any day we look at the news or see what is being said, done, or reported on the internet, it is not hard to see that the forces of evil are still on the loose. The transcendent God may be intimately involved in ongoing creative and providential care for all that is. Yet in a universe in which love is the central force, God has created persons capable not only of loving but (if love is to be meaningful) also capable of rebelling against that love. So the created universe is a domain in which God's love is at the center, yet evil is, in God's providence, permitted to run rampant until things will be set right.

———

Returning to the positive and redemptive aspects of this vision, the central point to take away is that, in contrast to the

---

[21]Richard F. Lovelace, *Dynamics of Spiritual Life: An Evangelical Theology of Renewal* (Downers Grove, IL: InterVarsity Press, 1979), 256.

materialistic pragmatic understandings that have been the default outlooks for so many in the modern world, the moral beauty of God, the beauty of perfect love manifested in Christ's sacrificial love, is at the heart of Edwards's vision of reality. Ultimately, unlike what it often seems in the bleak, materialistic world, evil does not reign. The greatest beauty is in redemptive love that brings the triumph of good over evil.

Theologian Edward Farley goes so far as to say that for Edwards, "beauty is more central and more pervasive than in any other text in the history of Christian theology."[22] As Edwards himself wrote, "God is God, and to be chiefly distinguished from all other beings, and exalted above them, chiefly by his divine beauty."[23] And the beauty that enthralls us—as Edwards often observes—is none other than God's love. In speaking of the purpose of creation, he says, there is an expression of "an infinite fullness of all possible goodness in God, a fullness of every perfection, of excellence and beauty, of every perfection." God has created the universe in order to share the Trinity's love with other persons who are capable of meaningful love.[24]

An important corollary of personal love and beauty at the center of reality is that recognizing it will spark joy and delight. In Edwards's rhapsody on the beauty of the flowers and the fields quoted earlier, he says: "So the green trees and fields, and singing of birds, are the emanations of his infinite joy and benignity."[25] The triune God of creation and redemption is a God of *joy*. The

---

[22]Edward Farley, *Faith and Beauty: A Theological Aesthetic* (Oxford: Routledge, 2001), 43, quoted in Lane, *Ravished*, 171.

[23]Jonathan Edwards, *Religious Affections*, ed. John E. Smith, *WJE* 2:298.

[24]Edwards's treatise "Concerning the End for Which God Created the World," in *Ethical Writings*, ed. Paul Ramsey, *WJE* 8, addresses this them.

[25]Edwards, Miscellany 108, in *Miscellanies a–500*, *WJE* 13:280.

highest joy is a joy of *mutual* love and delight. One of Edwards's favorite images is that of the church as the bride of Christ. That image suggests the unbounded delight that a bridegroom and bride have in each other. As Edwards expresses this in one of his sermons, "Christ and his church, like the bridegroom and bride, rejoice in each other, as in those that are the objects of each others' most tender and ardent love." He then quotes Zephaniah 3:17: "The LORD thy God in the midst of thee is mighty; he will save, he will rejoice over thee with joy; he will rest in his love, he will joy over thee with singing." He goes on to comment: "So the church, in the exercises of her love to Christ, rejoices with unspeakable joy."[26] The primary purpose for which the mighty God has created this universe, then, is so that creatures might live in the infinite pleasure of the joy of God's love.

———

Another of Edwards's favorite images for the ever-flowing beauty of God's love and joy is a fountain of *light*. God's light and love "flow forth, that the infinite fountain of good should send forth abundant streams, that this infinite fountain of light should, diffusing its excellent fullness, pour forth light all around."[27] In one of his meditations Edwards offers a further wonderful image for appreciating the impact of this fountain of light on the believer.

A man that sets himself to reason without divine light is like a man that goes in the dark into a garden full of the most beautiful plants, and most artfully ordered, and

---

[26]Jonathan Edwards, "The Church's Marriage to Her Sons and to Her God" (1746), in *Sermons and Discourses 1743–1758*, ed. Wilson H. Kimnach, *WJE* 25:180.
[27]Edwards, "End for Which God Created," *WJE* 8:433.

compares things together by going from one thing to another, to feel of them and to measure the distances; but he that sees by divine light is like a man that views the garden when the sun shines upon it.[28]

One could scarcely any better describe the difference in sensibility of the humblest Christian and the greatest modern secular scientist who hopes to master the world by measuring and ordering, yet who does so in the dark. C. S. Lewis offers a succinct version of much the same image when he says: "I believe in Christianity as I believe that the Sun has risen, not only because I see it, but because by it I see everything else."[29]

Edwards brought together these images of light most effectively in his famous sermon "A Divine and Supernatural Light." This was Edwards's greatest sermon and is the best place to start in reading Edwards himself. (See the appendix.) Preached to his congregation in Northampton in 1733, when Edwards was still a young pastor, he thought it important enough to have it published the next year. In this sermon he sounded some central themes for that most remarkable awakening that would overtake the town in 1734 and 1735.

By "a divine and supernatural light" Edwards means a gift of the Holy Spirit that illumines a believer's entire view of reality. For persons formerly living in the shadows, it is the wonderful light that illumines the beauty radiating from the love of God in Christ. Seeing by this "spiritual light," like any encounter with great beauty, changes one's deepest sensibilities. It awakens "a real

---

[28]Edwards, Miscellany 408, "Spiritual Knowledge," in *Miscellanies a–500*, *WJE* 13:470.

[29]C. S. Lewis, "Is Theology Poetry?" *Essays Collection and Other Short Pieces* (London: HarperCollins, 2000), 21.

sense of the excellency of God, and Jesus Christ, and of the work of redemption, and the ways and works of God revealed in the gospel." It is "a sense of the beauty, amiableness, or sweetness of a thing so that the heart is sensible of pleasure and delight" in it.

So he says, "There is a difference between having an opinion that God is holy and glorious, and having a sense of the loveliness and beauty of that holiness and grace. There is a difference between having a rational judgment that honey is sweet, and having a sense of its sweetness." Or

> there is a difference between believing that a person is beautiful, and having a sense of his [or her] beauty. The former may be obtained by hearsay, but the latter only by seeing the countenance. There is a wide difference between mere speculative rational judging any thing to be excellent, and having a sense of its sweetness and beauty. The former rests only in the head, speculation only is concerned in it; but the heart is concerned in the latter. When the heart is sensible of the beauty and amiableness of a thing, it necessarily feels pleasure in the apprehension.

When one sees the light, one is, as that "most reluctant convert" C. S. Lewis later put it, "surprised by joy." Or, in Edwards's words: "This knowledge is that which is above all others sweet and joyful." This "divine light shining into the soul . . . gives a view of those things that are immensely the most exquisitely beautiful, and capable of delighting the eye of the understanding. This spiritual light is the dawning of the light of glory in the heart."[30]

---

[30]Jonathan Edwards, "A Divine and Supernatural Light," in *Reader*, 111-12, 123. Also in the appendix of this book, pp. 143-44, 159.

Edwards's emphasis on this life-changing light was, of course, not unique to him but was a central image in the New Light awakenings of which he was a part and in the emerging evangelical movement. Just a few years later, as Methodists were sparking their own awakenings, Charles Wesley, for instance, similarly depicted the heart-changing thrill of such illumination in his great hymn "And Can It Be":

> Long my imprison'd spirit lay,
> Fast bound in sin and nature's night:
> Thine eye diffus'd a quick'ning ray;
> I woke; the dungeon flam'd with light;
> My chains fell off, my heart was free,
> I rose, went forth, and follow'd thee.[31]

Edwards in one of his meditations offers a beautifully gentle image reflecting on the ongoing love of Christ as like the light of the sun. The soul of a Christian, he says, is

> like the little white flower: pure, unspotted and undefined, low and humble, pleasing and harmless; receiving the beams, the pleasant beams of the serene sun, gently moved and a little shaken by a sweet breeze, rejoicing as it were in a calm rapture, diffusing around [a] most delightful fragrancy, standing most peacefully and lovingly in the midst of the other like flowers round.[32]

---

[31]Charles Wesley, "And Can It Be" (1738), also "Free Grace," in *Hymns and Sacred Poems* (London: Strahan, 1739), 117-19. See www.umc.org/en/content/and-can-it-be-that-i-should-gain-by-charles-wesley.
[32]Jonathan Edwards, "On Holiness," in *Miscellanies a–500*, *WJE* 13:663.

While Edwards enjoyed such contemplations in which he could bask in the beauty of Christ's love, and we may be inspired to such contemplations ourselves, it is also helpful to emphasize that Edwards did not see contemplation of the beauty of God's love as an end in itself. The experience of perceiving the love of Christ means that our own loves will be drawn to and shaped by that love. Bathed in that light, our hearts will grow toward actively loving Christ and others. Even the little flower that is basking in the sun of God's love is being energized by that sun and lovingly "diffusing its delightful fragrancy."

"Delightful" also reflects Edwards's emphasis that the experience of God's beauty is essentially *affective*—another of Edwards's most prominent emphases in describing the experience of the Christian life. That is in contrast to the detached and analytic approaches to reality that have characterized so much of modern thought. The greatest beauty that we can perceive is God's redemptive love in Christ. It is the beauty of the love of a person. In response, our hearts will be drawn to that person. Our deepest desires will be to truly love that person and what that person loves. And our deepest loves or affections will, of course, drive our actions.

Edwards's frequent use of the image of the light of the sun reminds us, then, that our encounters with the beauty of God's love are not just passive contemplative experiences. We are not just basking in perceiving Platonic perfections. When we perceive God's hand in the beauties of nature, it is not just like contemplating a great work of art—as exhilarating as that can be. When we experience the beauty of love, our response in return will be personal and active. Recognition of being loved will change our loves and affections. And our loves and affections are what direct our actions. So the beauty of Christ, even when appreciated through contemplation, is always in essence an *active beauty*, or a beauty that shapes our actions. As the sun is to the earth, the beauty of God's atoning love in Christ is the great dynamo that generates Christian action. The light of this love draws the soul entirely to Christ, and so "this light, and this light only, has its fruit in an universal holiness of life. . . . It draws forth the heart in a sincere love to God, which is the only principle of a true, gracious, and universal obedience."[33]

As Belden C. Lane observes in his insightful *Ravished by Beauty: The Surprising Legacy of Reformed Spirituality*, "Any Calvinistic spirituality worth its salt will make its way from aesthetic to ethics, from the celebration of God's beauty to the communication of it to others." So, he says, we should seek the "marriage of beauty and justice."[34] Justice is a type of beauty, restoring practices that are unfair, abusive, and distorted to their proper relationships. Recognizing and loving the light of beauty in one part of God's creation should motivate us to work to promote right relationships in every area that we can.

Elaine Scarry in her study *On Beauty and Being Just* makes a similar point, observing that in most eras and cultures beauty has been associated with harmonies, symmetry, and proper proportions. That was certainly the view of beauty in Edwards's day and his own view. And as Scarry argues, whatever may be our view of other sorts of beauty, these traits of the beauty of harmony

---

[33]Edwards, "Divine and Supernatural Light," 124. Also in the appendix of this book, p. 160.

[34]Lane, *Ravished*, 239 and 238. Dane C. Ortlund, *Edwards on the Christian Life: Alive to the Beauty of God* (Wheaton, IL: Crossway, 2014), is another particularly helpful guide to such themes.

and proportion are central to views of justice. So, for instance, she says, "Symmetry remains key, particularly in accounts of distributive justice and fairness 'as a symmetry of everyone's relation to one another.'"[35]

———

Edwards's view of God's love as overwhelming beauty is also a helpful way of explaining the paradox of God's grace and our choice—and hence our action. The Holy Spirit is the source of the change of heart that transforms us and our actions from being centered essentially around our self-loves to being able, even if imperfectly, to love Christ and what Christ loves. Yet this wholly gracious change of heart is in a real sense *our* act and the actions that follow from it are *our* choices. Both these seemingly contradictory things can be true if we truly appreciate the power of beauty. When we perceive something immensely beautiful, we cannot help but be drawn to it. We do not create our love for the beautiful person or for the beautiful thing that is the expression of that person. Our love is caused by the encounter. One might think, for example, of the most enthralling musical performance that you have ever heard, where you were simply overwhelmed with love for what you are hearing. Or, as we have seen, in "A Divine and Supernatural Light," Edwards uses the image of falling in love, of seeing a beautiful person whose actions and appearance manifest a great beauty of character and not being able to help loving that person. Yet even as the direction of our heart is irresistibly

---

[35]Elaine Scarry, *On Beauty and Being Just* (Princeton, NJ: Princeton University Press, 1999), 97.

transformed by such encounters, our response is still surely our own. It is *our* will that is acting according to our own deepest desires. In the transforming experience of knowing God, both God's action and our own response are necessary. The transforming work of the Holy Spirit is necessary for us to overcome our blinding preoccupations with our love to self. By God's grace, we are given eyes to see the wonderful beauty of Christ's transforming work. Yet our response to that beauty is surely our own voluntary choice.

Finally, we can further develop the image of the sun in relation to rightly ordering our loves in a further way. Not only does the sun light up everything else and so draw us to see the beauty around us, but the sun also keeps the planets in their orbits. We might think of our natural fallen state as like that of asteroids driven by the pulls of lesser loves into ultimately meaningless and destructive directions. But if we are drawn into the beauty of the powerful love of the triune God, that will, like the gravity of the sun, draw our selfish and lesser loves into their proper orbits. As James K. A. Smith has emphasized in *You Are What You Love* and his other outstanding books on being Augustinian Christians today, if God is our highest love, then that supreme love will properly order our lesser loves.[36] Edwards says much the same thing when he says that the Christian will love what God loves. That does not mean that our loves for lesser things—including even love of self—are obliterated. Rather it means that these are put into their proper places. So I find it helpful to pray something like this: that I may be given eyes to see the beauty of the astonishing sacrificial love of Christ that is

---

[36]James K. A. Smith, *You Are What You Love* (Grand Rapids, MI: Brazos, 2016).

the great light and dynamo at the heart of reality. And may the beauty of that love supreme draw me to it so that it may keep my other loves in their proper orbits. And knowing that, in fact, every day many of one's loves go flying off on their own is all the more reason to keep renewing such a prayer.

4

EDWARDS *and* *the* CHURCHES *That* WHITEFIELD BUILT

IT IS ONE thing to have a grand theological vision. It is another to be able to sustain that vision in real life. Anyone who has pursued high ideals knows how elusive they can be and how easily we can be distracted by our lesser interests, concerns, and sinfulness. We can be greatly blessed by great insights, yet we also know how imperfectly we actually apply them to our lives. That seems to be the case even for those who appear to be the greatest saints.

If that is the case for individuals, it is far more difficult for entire church communities over time and through cultural changes. The history of Christianity is littered with grand ideals and laudable reforms that sooner or later went astray. In each era and in each cultural setting, the lives of the people who make up the church are shaped by a multitude of customs, practices, assumptions, prejudices, legal systems, economic interests, government controls, affiliations, loyalties, and family and personal relationships. Each of these is touched only in part by specifically religious commitments. And when people who have not been previously churched are brought to the faith, they come not only with the universal frailties and needs of human nature but also with all sorts of culturally conditioned traits. Many of these traits can be appropriately transformed by the faith and turned toward the good. Christianity has proven itself amazingly adaptable in countless cultural settings. Yet the promises of the gospel are directed toward the weak rather than the strong. The church is, after all, for sinners. It is an institution where flawed people can gather together. Some remain very needy. Some muddle along as best they can. Some may be self-deluded. Some may perpetuate unhealthy traits, prejudices, and practices in the name of Christianity. Some may just go along with family or community expectations. Many are sincerely dedicating their lives to Christ and trying to do the best they can but remain, like the rest of us, flawed in many respects. In theological terms, sanctification is incomplete even for the best of Christians.

So it is hardly surprising that church communities often fail to challenge some of the cultural idols, prejudices, and practices prevalent in their time and place. That is not to say that they should not be trying all the more to identify such shortcomings and to correct them. Rather it is to say that, historically speaking, we should not be surprised when we find so many examples of these preexisting cultural traits, biases, or idols transforming the faith, often in subtle ways. And having been alerted to such tendencies, we can be in a better position to counter them constructively.

The twentieth-century ethicist Reinhold Niebuhr offered very helpful insights on the almost universal human tendency for our best accomplishments to lead to paradoxical consequences.

Niebuhr observed that there seemed to be a sinful principle built into human nature, leading us to think too highly of ourselves. So our virtues often turn into our vices. A great athlete may come to be obsessed with physical prowess. A person of great intellect may disdain people of lesser intelligence. A great artist or musician may have no time for people of lesser abilities. A great preacher might get carried away by his or her power. A great nation or political party may champion freedom and justice but promote their virtuous goals by means that bring oppression and injustice.

As a historian of American Christianity, one of my principal concerns has been to understand how these often-paradoxical interactions of culture and faith have shaped churches, especially Protestant churches in America, over the centuries. The stories of those churches have been in many ways success stories. Rates of churchgoing in America have long been remarkably high, especially when compared with other countries of the former Christendom, such as those of Western Europe. And twenty-first-century American churchgoing rates, despite recent declines, are still considerably higher than they were in colonial times. Further, over the past two centuries American efforts have been among the factors that helped spark the indigenous spread of Christianity in many parts of the Majority World. For these successes, we must give credit first of all to the work of the Holy Spirit. Yet as Richard Lovelace emphasizes throughout his *Dynamics of Spiritual Life,* the Holy Spirit always works in specific cultural contexts of which we need to be aware. Furthermore, as Edwards himself notes, Satan is working to subvert true awakenings by promoting deceptive imitations. So as limited humans we must use great caution, recognizing that we cannot know exactly what God's purposes are or how those purposes might be interacting with the invisible counterforces of evil.

————

In the 1740s and 1750s, the two most famous men in America were Benjamin Franklin and George Whitefield. By the 1750s Franklin was being celebrated not only for his electrical experiences and some practical inventions but also as a highly successful publisher, the author of the popular (though pseudonymous) *Poor Richard's Almanac*, Pennsylvania's leading citizen, its representative to Great Britain, and the first leader to propose a union of the colonies. Despite all that, George Whitefield was much more widely known, having been seen personally by far more people than anyone else in America.

In fact, though Whitefield confined his preaching tours to Great Britain and its American colonies, he may have been seen in his day by more people than anyone else in the world. Though he continued to reside principally in England, he had by the 1750s already made five arduous journeys to America. Beginning with his second visit from 1739 to 1740, Whitefield, still only in his midtwenties, preached almost daily as he traveled up and down the Atlantic Seaboard. He preached thousands of times, often out-of-doors and often to crowds that included a good percentage of the population in the region. In Boston in 1740, for instance, he stayed for four weeks, sometimes preaching to crowds of five to eight thousand. This was when the entire population of the city was something like fifteen thousand.

When he would move on to a new region, he made sure there would be advance publicity. During the height of what became known as a colonial-wide "great awakening," just about anyone who could came out to hear him. One famous account comes from a farmer in Massachusetts who, when he heard that Whitefield was soon going to preach nearby, dropped his farming tools, grabbed his horse and his wife, and breathlessly joined a sort of stampede of people and horses hurrying to get to the preaching site.[1] Whitefield was the first American superstar. He was a great dramatist.[2] His voice could be heard clearly from long distances and could charm a crowd.

When Edwards heard of Whitefield's successes in the middle colonies and that he was planning to come to New England, he eagerly wrote to him in February 1740 to ensure that the evangelist would include Northampton in his visit. Edwards viewed Whitefield as, quite literally, a godsend. The amazing awakening of 1734 and 1735 in Northampton had cooled. Edwards was deeply concerned about the backsliding into old ways of many who had been touched by the awakening. A visit from Whitefield might re-ignite the revival fires. Though Whitefield was ordained in the Church of England, he was known to be thoroughly Reformed in his theology. So the two evangelists shared very similar goals and perspective for the revival of the churches.

Whitefield knew of Edwards from "A Faithful Narrative" and was glad to accept the invitation. And when he came to

---

[1] It is a fascinating, brief read: George Leon Walker, *Some Aspects of the Religious Life of New England* (New York: Silver, Burnett, and Company, 1897), 89-92. Cited in "The Great Awakening Comes to Weathersfield, Connecticut," History Matters (website), http://historymatters.gmu.edu/d/5711.

[2] Harry S. Stout, *The Divine Dramatist: George Whitefield and the Rise of Modern Evangelicalism* (Grand Rapids, MI: Eerdmans, 1991).

preach in Northampton in the summer of 1740, the impressive young evangelist indeed helped spark what became a second revival. In fact revival fires spread in New England in a "great and general awakening." Whitefield's visit to the Edwards home in 1740 also seems to have been a success on a personal level. He was especially impressed by the demeanor of the large Edwards household. At the time there were seven children. The three oldest, Sarah, Jerusha, and Esther, ages twelve to eight, responded especially well to a meeting with the evangelist. Whitefield said of Jonathan and Sarah that "a sweeter couple I have never seen," and he was especially awestruck by Sarah for her piety and demeanor. After the visit, the twenty-five-year-old bachelor wrote in his diary, "I have put to God, that He would be pleased to send me a daughter of Abraham to be my wife."[3]

In the light of such a good start in the relationship between Whitefield and Edwards, it may be a bit of a surprise to learn that in the long run Whitefield became a closer friend of Benjamin Franklin than of Edwards. In part that might be explained by Philadelphia being a thriving port that Whitefield often visited. Northampton was on the frontier in distant western Massachusetts. Still, Edwards and Whitefield did not keep up a correspondence, and the closer friendship with Franklin provides at least a symbolic entry into understanding Whitefield's legacy for the American churches.

Whitefield and Franklin were in many ways two of an emerging new kind: the self-made man. There had always

---

[3]George Whitefield, journal entry, October 19, 1740, in *George Whitefield's Journals* (Edinburgh: Banner of Truth, 1960), 476-77.

occasionally been men and women who broke through the boundaries of status and hierarchies. But with the technological innovations available by the eighteenth century, that was becoming more common, especially for White men. Mobility of travel provided many new opportunities for both Whitefield and Franklin. And the printing press gave the self-educated Franklin a voice stronger than that of most intellectual elites. Whitefield also used the press effectively to publicize and recount his travels and successes. Meanwhile some of the cultural and intellectual changes of the time were beginning to foster widespread questioning of traditional hierarchies and authorities. In America, everything was relatively new, inherited nobility was rare, and there were few strong institutional authorities. So all these trends were accelerated. Soon Americans would be talking about "the rights of man," and the self-made man would become one of the most celebrated American ideals.

Whitefield and Franklin were both innovators and admired each other's successes. Early on in Whitefield's first American tour, Franklin attended one of the evangelist's outdoor meetings in Philadelphia. Franklin was impressed by Whitefield's striking oratory and walked back as far as he could to measure the distance at which he could still be heard. Calculating from that, he estimated that the young preacher could be heard by thirty thousand people at one time.[4] But Franklin was also listening to the sermon, and by its end he was convinced to donate to the orphanage in Georgia that Whitefield was supporting. According to Franklin's later story, he had come with empty pockets to

---

[4]Thomas S. Kidd, *George Whitefield: America's Spiritual Founding Father* (New Haven, CT: Yale University Press, 2014), 84-85.

prevent such an eventuality but then borrowed from an acquaintance in order to donate.

Franklin was not conventionally religious himself, but he believed that conventional religion had practical benefits for society. It was especially useful for helping to suppress the worst vices of the common people and to teach them to obey lawful authority. Beyond that, conventional religion had the measurable good effect for society, as in the case of Whitefield's orphanage, of encouraging acts of charity and good works, ideals for which Franklin had genuine concern. Whitefield doubtless honored such charitable sentiments and, seeing the advantages of an alliance with a publicist and leading citizen of such influence, reciprocated the friendship. Whitefield stayed in Franklin's home when he visited Philadelphia on later occasions, and the two corresponded. In 1756, Franklin, who was always looking for great new projects, even suggested that the two might cooperate in founding a new colony in the Ohio territory.

It is hardly surprising, then, that Whitefield brought to the job of revitalizing the American churches many approaches similar to those that Franklin brought to building a new culture and nation. These innovative principles proved invaluable in fostering the vast successes of evangelical Christianity in America. Whitefield preached what has become a classic evangelical message, emphasizing the Bible as the sole authority and conversion through trusting in the atoning work of Jesus on the cross. Many Black churches, as well as those of predominantly White or just about every other ethnic constituency, have thrived on preaching variations on the same themes that Whitefield helped popularize.

And even more remarkably, by the twenty-first century, variations of evangelical Christianity have spread to just about every part of the world. In many parts of Africa and Asia the numbers of people who attend such churches far surpass the numbers of active Christians in almost every part of the former Christendom. As historian Mark Noll has argued, looking at evangelicalism in the United States offers us insight into the world movement, and not primarily because of direct American influences. The United States in its early years was the first modern nation. It was relatively free from strong traditional institutions and especially open to new technology and innovations. The evangelicalism that burgeoned into the dominant American religious style thus often became a sort of prototype for vital Protestant Christianity in modernizing settings throughout the world.[5] The American story is also unique in a number of important ways, especially in having dominant Protestant influences during its earliest formative years and also having religious diversity. Recognizing both its typical character and its uniqueness, we can here look at evangelicalism as it emerged in America and at the same time offer readers from any culture some examples of the challenges that face Christians in the modern world.

———

We can begin with two related traits of the new evangelicalism emerging in the eighteenth century: distrust of established institutional authority and increasing trust in individual experience.

---

[5]Mark A. Noll, *The New Shape of World Christianity: How American Experience Reflects Global Faith* (Downers Grove, IL: IVP Academic, 2009).

Those traits are evident in the two men who did the most to shape evangelicalism as a major movement in the English-speaking world, George Whitefield and John Wesley. Both were ordained Anglicans, but each effectively ignored most formal church authority. If they were not invited to preach in churches, they preached to far larger crowds outdoors in the fields. They established their own itineraries, networks, and publications. Wesley built an elaborate formal network of Methodist societies, technically within the Anglican Church but really under his personal leadership and guidance. These amounted to a separate denomination and after Wesley's death became recognized as such. Wesley also introduced some theological innovations that were variations on the Arminian emphasis on the ability of individuals freely to choose to follow Christ. Wesley also emphasized the discernible role of the Holy Spirit in the experiences of ongoing sanctification. And even though these differences led Whitefield and Wesley, who had once been close friends, to go their separate ways, the emerging evangelical movement would continue to display many family resemblances. Both Whitefield and Wesley emphasized personal experiences of conversion and lives shaped by disciplines of holiness and practices of charity. And even their readiness to go their separate ways was a harbinger of what have been some major tendencies of evangelicalism: to favor strong, inspiring, individual leadership over institutional tradition, to divide over differing doctrines and practices, and to grow through splitting.

In emphasizing individual experience more than relying on instituted authorities and rituals, Whitefield, Wesley, and their followers and imitators in the awakenings were expressing new emphases on the individual that had been gradually appearing throughout the European world. Philosopher Charles Taylor argues that prior to the mid-1600s, European thought had not placed much emphasis on "the self."[6] Religious movements were important contributors to an increasing role of the self in shaping one's own identity. Throughout history, the identities of most people had been defined primarily by the communities to which they belonged and by the status they were born into in those communities. Christianity itself was revolutionary, when it first spread throughout the Roman world, in that it taught that anyone's primary identity could be shaped by one's beliefs and commitments as well as by one's status. And it even taught that belief and commitment could be more important than status and that the poor and the weak had special standing in the divine regime.[7] In later medieval Christendom, while these revolutionary ethical teachings continued to be found, Christian identity was most often inherited as part of one's cultural identity, as signaled by infant baptism and christening. And status differences remained strong. Protestantism, by challenging centralized church authority and by emphasizing the importance of individual faith, helped open the door for a new emphasis on the role of the individual in the modern era. Edwards's precursors, the early American Puritans, offer a telling example. Even though they themselves were authoritarian in many ways, they were ready to challenge established English authorities of

---

[6]Charles Taylor, *Sources of the Self and the Making of Modern Identity* (Cambridge, MA: Harvard University Press, 1989).

[7]Tom Holland, *Dominion: How the Christian Revolution Remade the World* (New York: Basic Books, 2019), tells the story of the revolutionary nature of Christianity in helping to reshape the world.

church and state and to risk their lives to protect their independence. And they tempered the authoritarianism of their government of both state and church with some recognition of the role of the governed in choosing their own authorities. Another particularly important trait was that, while the Puritans strongly emphasized communal identity and institutional authority, they were also notorious for encouraging self-examination. All people were to examine their individual spiritual condition to see whether they truly belonged to the highest of their communities. Being a full member of the church was not simply something one was born and baptized into.

Some in the Puritan movement became Baptists who carried the emphasis on individual choice a step further, insisting that baptism was only for professing adults. Often that stance involved rejecting state religion entirely. In the colonies, Roger Williams was the best-known example. Williams rejected as unbiblical the whole idea of Christendom. Churches, he said, are voluntary associations of individuals and should be free from state control. While in the 1600s Baptists remained a radical minority, the awakenings beginning in the 1700s helped them take root in the American colonies. Such religious emphases on the individual flourished in the American setting, where social mobility and status were more fluid than in the Old World. By the early 1800s Baptists had become the largest Protestant grouping in the United States.

The Puritan movement in England and New England was just one part of the ongoing breakup of Christendom since the Reformation. Part of the problem, as Baptists pointed out, was that after the Reformation the assumption persisted that Christian rulers should support a state church that taught the one true religion. Early Lutheran and Calvinist Reformation movements depended on the support of local princes for survival. Catholic rulers preserved Catholic churches. Europe, as a result, had been thrown into a long period of terrible warfare, typically with religious dimensions. In kingdoms such as England and France, it was for a long time not certain whether the monarch—and hence the whole territory—would be Protestant or Catholic. In England the Elizabethan compromise of the later 1500s established the Anglican state church, combining Protestant doctrine with some traditional Catholic practices. That led to the rise of the Puritan movement, which advocated for a more thoroughgoing Calvinist Reformation. By the 1640s that dissent, with strong Presbyterian counterparts in Scotland, brought a civil war and the first modern revolution with the execution of King Charles I in 1649. The ensuing commonwealth era, lasting until 1660, not only brought Puritan rule but a proliferation of more radical Protestant sects.

Even though the British monarchy was restored in 1660 and the Puritan party was suppressed, it was becoming impossible for the state to maintain religious uniformity. In 1688 the "Glorious Revolution," as the Protestants called it, replaced King James II, a Catholic, with Protestants William and Mary of Orange. By now, it was clear throughout Great Britain and its colonies that, even though there could still be state churches, they would have to at least tolerate some other varieties of religious groups.

Another problem of state churches is that such official top-down religion can lead to spiritual deadness. One response to that phenomenon was the rise in Continental Europe, beginning in the later 1600s, of Pietist renewal movements, especially among Lutherans in the various German states. Pietists emphasized conversion, personal religious commitment, evangelism, missions, and practices of holiness and charity. Such concerns had parallels in Puritan New England of the same era. Cotton Mather, the most prominent Puritan writer in the generation before Edwards, corresponded with some of the German Pietist leaders. And the awakenings in New England churches of that time, as promoted by Solomon Stoddard, Timothy Edwards, and others, can be seen as comparable renewal efforts. By Jonathan Edwards's generation, Pietism would be directly helping to shape what would become known as the evangelical movement among the British. In the 1730s John Wesley was deeply influenced by the piety of some Moravian missionaries whom he met. Under the leadership of Count Nicholas von Zinzendorf, the Moravians had recently become one of the most active European groups promoting the new piety and missions. Wesley, Whitefield, and others would foster British equivalents of Pietist concerns for religious renewal.

The British colonies of the New World were especially ripe for such awakenings, since most traditional institutions were relatively weak. With almost no formal nobility and lots of economic opportunities, status and social standing were in flux. Though almost every White person had a Christian heritage, frontier conditions could be rough and disorienting. Churches, especially when strengthened by religious renewal, could be important factors in shaping individual lives and in building communities.

Whitefield's New Light message resonated not only with the emerging emphasis on individual choice but also with another, related modern trend: to confirm one's beliefs by empirical verification. And, in an era when traditional authorities were coming into question—and in regions where traditional institutions were weak—one way of testing a claim is by relying on direct personal experience. That is, after all, the way that we commonly form our beliefs: in interpersonal relationships. We learn to trust other persons through our direct experiences with them. And since Christianity is essentially about personal relationships to the divine, that made sense as a way of testing what was authentic faith. So at the same time in the eighteenth century when "enlightened" proponents of more rational Christianity were looking for more scientific or objective evidence of what might authenticate reliable religious belief, the evangelists of the new awakenings emphasized that one must authenticate faith by direct personal experience of God's grace in Christ.

Whitefield deserves credit for being one of the first and most effective in adapting the presentation of the gospel to these new circumstances. He is rightly celebrated as one of the founders of the evangelical style of Christianity that can still be seen flourishing in much of the world. The British American colonies, where forces of modernity and mobility had been weakening traditions and authorities, were the regions where this religious style first put down its deepest roots. Through the next centuries, evangelical forms of Christianity proved adaptable to all sorts of other changing, modern circumstances and brought a gospel message to many other parts of the world where traditional cultures and communities had been weakening.

———

As observed earlier in this chapter, even the greatest human accomplishments typically have paradoxical downsides, and often the best of human endeavors have downsides of unintended consequences. So the very innovations that have been most helpful in advancing Christ's kingdom in modern or postmodern times may also turn out to undermine parts of the Christian witness. We can here reflect on some of those paradoxes.

One such mixed blessing has been the rise of celebrity culture. The breakdown of strict class distinctions and of inherited authority opened the door to the rise of talented celebrities to become some of the dominating figures in modern cultures. Christianity itself has long cultivated regard for the lowborn, and inspiring leaders whose talents and effectiveness made them famous were nothing new in the history of the church. But in the emerging modern era, George Whitefield was among the first and most effective in mobilizing the new media and technologies for promoting himself. As a self-made man, he was not dependent on family status nor on strong institutions. It is important to note, though, that Whitefield's self-promotion was duly and often sacrificially subordinated to promoting the larger cause of the gospel. Yet almost immediately his successes inspired imitators, some of whom were not always so scrupulous. In the American colonies, for instance, Whitefield's sensational preaching tour from 1739 to 1740 immediately led to many imitators. Itinerant preachers crisscrossed the settlements hoping to carry on Whitefield's work. One way to draw crowds was to preach a message that was sensationally radical. Edwards, who was one of New England's leading defenders of the awakenings, nonetheless recognized that some of the awakeners' efforts to excite emotion led to excesses. He in fact had to help deal personally with New England's most sensational cases. James Davenport, a young enthusiast, became notorious for, among other extravagances, building bonfires and then urging his followers to throw in and burn their theological books and fine clothes. On at least a couple of occasions Davenport was declared by local authorities to be certifiably insane. Critics of the awakenings, such as the formidable Boston Congregational pastor Charles Chauncy, argued that such excesses proved that the awakenings would lead to spiritual anarchy. Edwards countered that, despite admitted excesses, there were too many other cases of people being truly converted to allow rejection of the whole movement. Blanket condemnations such as Chauncy's might stop the excesses, but they would also hinder the responsible evangelists and so stop some of the proven workings of the Holy Spirit. Edwards saw the solution as to continue to promote the awakeners but then to make some careful distinctions so as to be able to tell the difference between authentic religious faith and its counterfeits.

Before we consider the merits of recovering Edwards's balanced approach, we need also to recognize that Charles Chauncy had a point. Speaking for much of the Massachusetts Congregational Church leadership, he was raising the question of what would happen if the New Light evangelicals took over and anyone who could draw a crowd as a preacher could simply bypass traditional church authority and theological restraints. Would not the triumph of New Light evangelicalism lead to anarchy? Looking back from the twenty-first century, that is indeed what often has happened. Even as a gospel message much like Whitefield's has spread remarkably in the United States and elsewhere, it has often been accompanied by many excesses. Once we consider why both evangelical successes and evangelical aberrations are still very much with us, we can appreciate why Edwards remains such a helpful guide for sorting out the differences.

Closely related to the rise of celebrity culture was increased dependence on the market. With the decline of state-supported religion and increased emphasis on individual choice, evangelists increasingly emphasized presenting the gospel message attractively to new audiences. The eighteenth century was a time of flourishing of the new market economy in the British and European world, moving beyond more localized agrarian economies of earlier eras. Religious innovators like the Wesleys and Whitefield were resourceful innovators in moving beyond parish boundaries and also in applying new techniques of publicity and promotion, and hence marketing, in the interest of religious renewal. John Wesley, for instance, developed an impressively efficient system for training and mobilizing a large network of evangelists. Whitefield became a master at promoting his preaching using the newly popular newspapers for advance publicity, enhancing his celebrity status. As a former student of the stage, he applied techniques of the theater to preaching, as in dramatizing the telling of Scripture stories in heart-melting ways. He was also a spectacularly compelling orator. Once again, one should admire such zeal and resourcefulness in promoting the gospel. Effective evangelism can be made much more effective by resourceful marketing. Yet a style of religion that is dependent on the market—on what works or what sells—clearly has the downside that it seems to invite religious anarchy.

Indeed, in the United States, where both economic and religious free markets flourished, the competitive style invited many innovators. Some of these based their appeal on innovative departures from the Christian mainstream. So in nineteenth-century America we find a burgeoning of competitive religious marketing that included a number of flourishing eccentric sectarian religious movements, such as the Mormons, Shakers, Adventists, Oneida Community, and Jehovah's Witnesses. Usually such new movements were built around one especially inspiring and resourceful leader who offered creative new outlooks and promises that appealed to a segment of the community that was bewildered by the competing claims of more mainstream groups and so open to something new and seemingly definitive.

Meanwhile, mainstream American evangelical Protestantism was dividing into scores of denominations. Most of these retained, as in Whitefield's time, a recognizable family resemblance in that they affirmed the Bible as the supreme authority and preached variations of the gospel of sin and salvation through the saving work of Christ on the cross. Yet, inevitably in a market economy, some would appeal to a few simple themes that might have wide, popular appeal.

Even within much of more conventional modern evangelicalism, one of the unintended consequences of jettisoning church traditions and authorities, as Whitefield helped introduce, was a change in the meaning of the Reformation maxim of "the Bible alone."

Whitefield and most of the other founders of evangelicalism had inherited the ideal of "the Bible alone" from Martin Luther, John Calvin, and other Reformers of two centuries earlier. The Reformers were convinced that the medieval church as ruled by the Roman papacy had been corrupted. The papacy protected itself from criticism by claiming a monopoly on interpreting authoritative church traditions. The Reformers countered that church teachings and traditions had to be tested by whether they were consistent with the highest authority, the original biblical teachings. So, while they accepted many church traditions and teachings as useful guides, they all were subject to the Bible alone, rather than the papacy, as the highest authority.

The Reformers such as Luther and Calvin had no intention that "the Bible alone" would mean that the church would abandon its best interpretive traditions or encourage untrained individuals to decide what the Bible meant without expert guidance. Luther's rebellion was that of a biblical scholar who was hoping to establish an authoritative orthodoxy that would be the basis for a united Christendom. His scholarship was, moreover, not just of his own devising but rather based on centuries of biblical interpretation going back to Augustine and other early church fathers. Many of the other leaders of the mainstream Protestant Reformation were likewise highly accomplished scholars of whom John Calvin became the most influential prototype. The intention of these leading Reformers was not to break up Christendom but rather to unite it on the basis of more reliable authority. Not only did they honor the ecumenical creeds of the ancient church, but they also carefully constructed updated creeds in order to distinguish the best of the tradition from what they considered to be Roman Catholic and other heresies. Probably they sometime erred in the direction of a too-exclusive doctrinal precision. Yet their fundamental instincts were sound. To keep the reforms of the church and the principle of "the Bible alone" from spinning off into a myriad of amateur private interpretations, they looked to try to find the best consensus among the trained experts who knew the ancient languages and were familiar with the long history of interpretations.

One biblical principle that such an approach reflected is that found in 1 Corinthians 12: the church as the body of Christ is made up of many parts, so it is essential for members to recognize that they need each other's gifts. Many gifts of the Spirit—such as faith, hope, and charity, for instance—are much higher than scholarship. Yet at the same time biblical scholars and theologians can play essential roles in keeping the church from going off track. Fallible as scholars may be, they still provide the best means for keeping church doctrines within the bounds of the best interpretations of biblical teaching that have stood the test of time.

Jonathan Edwards was heir to this formidable scholarly tradition. He saw himself not as just a New England Congregational pastor but more basically as part of an impressive international Reformed movement that for two centuries had been putting its best intellectual resources into showing the way to the true reform of Christendom. So Edwards could begin his theological inquiries at an already-high level, drawing on the works of a host of international Reformed scholastic theologians. One of the conspicuous traits of Reformed churches was their highly educated clergy. So, for example, despite limited resources, one of the first things that the Puritan settlers in New England did was to establish Harvard College in 1636. The literacy and education levels in the Puritan settlements were probably higher per capita than in any other region of the world. Leading Puritan clergy, including Edwards's grandfather and predecessor in Northampton, Solomon Stoddard, published sophisticated debates on theological and practical church matters. Though Edwards, like Stoddard, spent most of his career as a local pastor, it was fitting that his career should culminate in Princeton as president of the College of New Jersey, an institution dedicated first of all to training New Light clergy.

George Whitefield and John Wesley were both educated men who could take for granted the long theological heritage of the church going back to the church fathers. But their practical innovations, while immensely valuable in many respects, also had the unintended effect of inviting freelance imitators without such training who might distort the core message. As with most things, there were tradeoffs involved. Lay preaching has been an effective means to spread the gospel to many who have needed it.[8] Many talented people who were not privileged with opportunities for higher education have proved to be among the most highly effective evangelists and pastors. Even in the early days of evangelicalism, some of its preachers were women and persons of less privileged racial, ethnic, economic, or educational backgrounds. Such breaking down of what had been a monopoly for elite White males had much to recommend it and eventually became one of the great strengths of evangelical

---

[8]John Wesley recognized this issue and fostered quick basic training for people who would be clergy, yet they would remain under centralized church control.

Christianity. Yet, like so many good things, such innovations had a downside. In America, where traditions were weak and anti-intellectualism has been strong, depending on what succeeds best in the popular market has sometimes led to bypassing some of the checks and balances that have proven vital for the wider body of Christ. Through the centuries, mainstream Christian traditions had developed ways of ensuring that their teachings would remain consistent with what they understood to be mainstream Christian traditions, sound biblical interpretations, and the gospel message. Often that involved considerable educational requirements for clergy. Yet such traditions demanded time and resources that would slow evangelism and were not well suited to trying to keep up with the rapidly expanding American frontier.

We can get a good glimpse historically of the strengths and the weaknesses of evangelical zeal for "the Bible alone" if we look at American evangelicalism in the era after the American Revolution. During that time, even more than during the first Great Awakening of the colonial era, evangelical Christianity really began to take root in America. Particularly the more popular brands of conversionist Protestantism, as represented by Methodists and Baptists, spread to just about every American community. Historian Nathan O. Hatch in an especially helpful study characterized the second era of American awakenings as *The Democratization of American Christianity*.[9] As the American

------

[9]Nathan O. Hatch, *The Democratization of American Christianity* (New Haven, CT: Yale University Press, 1989).

Revolution had popularized the idea that democratic authority comes from the people, so the burgeoning American churches appealed to the common person rather than to inherited or state-supported institutional authority. So pervasive was the spread of this sort of revivalist Protestant faith in nineteenth-century America that by 1835 Alexis de Tocqueville, the great French observer of American democracy, could observe that "in the United States the sovereign authority is religious, and consequently hypocrisy must be common, but there is no country in the world where the Christian religion retains a greater influence over the souls of men than in America."[10]

One prominent tendency among the competing popular versions of evangelicalism that spread so remarkably on the American frontier was what scholars have called primitivist versions of Christianity. When the American nation was founded, its motto (still on the dollar bill) was "a new order for the ages." Many Americans of that era and since have similarly become convinced that the church needs to be reinvented, freeing itself of past corruptions. In the case of churches, a widely popular argument for how to get rid of those corruptions was to say that the Protestant principle of "the Bible alone" meant that we should simply return to the practices of the primitive New Testament church. For many, that seemed a commonsensical way to recapture the essence of Christianity, skipping all the intervening history, oppressive institutions, and often-contradictory theological interpretations. It also could appeal to the common sense of the common person. In the United States

---

[10]Alexis de Tocqueville, *Democracy in America,* trans. Henry Reeve, vol. 2 (1835; repr., New York: Vintage Books, 1955), 303.

the most explicit expressions of such primitivist views were found in the Disciples of Christ and related Churches of Christ or Christian Churches. Founded by Alexander Campbell and Barton Stone in the early 1800s, these generically named churches proposed to reunite all of Christendom on original New Testament principles. Many of the churches of the burgeoning Baptist movement of the same time likewise affirmed such primitivist aspirations, and they typically insisted that churches did not need formal creeds.

As such versions of evangelicalism spread, one popular implication was that "the Bible alone" often came to be seen as meaning that the Bible is the only thing a layperson needs to properly understand Christianity. Effective evangelists could quote impressive arrays of texts to support their views and then also encourage people to sit down with the Bible and "see for yourself" if those teachings were not indeed found there.

Much of American evangelicalism was becoming populist in its tendencies. Revivalist Christianity, after all, emphasized *individual* choice in conversion and commitment. And, more broadly, populist Christianity shapes its appeal to ordinary people. It is democratic in the sense of depending on the will of the people who adopt its message. At the same time, in actual practice, populist authority usually comes from the top down. Sometimes such centralized authority is frankly built into an ecclesiastical system. In the early American republic, that was especially true of the immensely successful Methodists. Methodist bishops oversaw a cadre of efficiently trained and organized evangelists, including many circuit riders who could spread their message on the frontier. But often in the wide-open American environment, top-down authority arises in a more truly populist fashion. The evangelists who succeed best are those who can attract the largest audiences and then build their own empires, usually offering simplified brands of the gospel that focus on a few compelling points with wide appeal. While Whitefield combined unusual talent with a gospel message grounded in a substantial theological tradition, many later populist evangelists have built their ministries with a message of "the Bible alone" that highlighted *their own* interpretations of the Bible. Often these emphases might be frankly anti-intellectual, disparaging the outlooks of the highly educated and the experts.

In the twentieth and twenty-first centuries, some of the clearest examples of the dangers of populist-based versions of Christianity can be seen in the widespread prosperity gospel. The Pentecostal tradition in which prosperity teachings have arisen is itself a prominent example of modern primitivist Christianity. While earlier versions of primitivism had promoted a return to the teachings and practices of the New Testament church, Pentecostals went a step further. They taught that modern Christians should participate in the same sorts of miraculous experiences as in New Testament times, such as speaking in tongues, dramatic healings, and other miraculous answers to prayer and divine interventions in their lives. The prosperity gospel goes beyond such teachings by combining biblical promises of answers to prayer with modern aspirations for wealth and material comforts. Resourceful leaders, who themselves may live extravagant lifestyles, can enhance their authority by claiming special revelations. And often prosperity preachers' own wealth is seen as illustrating the possibilities in God's promises. Pentecostal religion comes in many varieties, most of which avoid such excesses. Nonetheless, the prosperity gospel offers telling examples of where populism in a free market religious economy can lead.[11]

It is easy to point out excesses and dubious teachings in many of the manifestations of contemporary evangelicalism divorced from intellectually strong interpretive traditions. One pattern to note particularly is how market-driven evangelicalism is especially susceptible to being co-opted by populist agendas, including popular political agendas. That has become a conspicuous issue in our twenty-first-century era of political polarization, instant information, and misinformation.[12] Yet whatever our take on these and many other highly contested issues, we should be careful not to be too dismissive. We need to offer critiques (and sometimes strong critiques) of the aberrations that arise. Far too often captivating leaders use the gospel message for personal aggrandizement, to reinforce social and political prejudices, or as a cover for sexual abuses and abuses of power. Charles Chauncy had a point in saying that freewheeling evangelism would open the doors to disturbing aberrations. Still, Edwards had a telling counterpoint in insisting that that is not the whole story. We should not reject the entire evangelical tradition just because it sometimes leads to false teachings and scandals. So has every other tradition and institution, whether religious or secular, in human history. We do not condemn the

---

[11]See Kate Bowler, *Blessed: A History of the American Prosperity Gospel* (New York: Oxford University Press, 2013) for a helpful account and assessment.

[12]See the essays in Mark A. Noll, David W. Bebbington, and George M. Marsden, *Evangelicals: Who They Have Been, Are Now, and Could Be* (Grand Rapids, MI: Eerdmans, 2019) for a helpful variety of analysis and comment.

whole institution of motherhood, for instance, because some mothers abuse or abandon their children. But the proper response to abuses is to expose and root out the abuses so as to allow the good parts of the institutions to develop at their best. Abuses and scandals make news because they are not the norms. As Edwards argued, to dismiss the entire movement would be to thwart the work of the Holy Spirit in the many instances where the Spirit has worked through evangelical means to change and to shape the lives of some who are evidently saints by any Christian standard.

———

On the positive side, one of the most remarkable features in the history of modern evangelicalism is that, despite this often-freewheeling religious market economy with all its dubious innovations, the core gospel message that George Whitefield would recognize has survived. That basic gospel message endures in this market economy because it speaks to perennial human needs and so retains its potency and appeal. Even in the often-chaotic state of contemporary Christianity that the free market fosters, the Holy Spirit continues to speak in offering to needy sinners a gospel that is the revolutionary message of God's love manifested in Christ's sacrifice on the cross. In evangelical versions of Christianity that so strongly emphasize the authority of the Bible and especially the New Testament, one of the messages that continues to come through from the Bible itself is that God has taken on our weakness and suffering in Christ's atoning work. One might think that without the strengths of centralized church authority, sound scholarship, and authoritative creeds, this core message might get lost. Yet, even if it is frequently obscured by other concerns in often-unruly evangelicalism, it also remains one of the most common features. If the Bible is highly revered, preached, and studied, that basic gospel message is difficult to miss. And that basic message remains compelling in speaking to the human condition in every era and in every tribe and nation.

Turning once again to Richard Lovelace in his classic *Dynamics of Spiritual Life*, we can find some further wise advice for thinking of the relationship of the historically rooted theological traditions and the less rooted but more dynamic evangelical movements of our day. Given that the body of Christ is so irretrievably divided institutionally, Lovelace observes we nonetheless can do more to take seriously that *spiritually* the body of Christ is still united. Granted that, as Edwards himself would emphasize, Satan often countered true awakenings by producing similar but counterfeit religious movements that appealed to humans' self-loves. Yet Lovelace adds that at the same time we should recognize that the Holy Spirit typically uses imperfect teachings and practices (and that includes our own) to transform sinners and bring them into the kingdom. Heresies typically involve taking some valuable truth too far or emphasizing it too exclusively. So, rather than just dismissing those professing Christians with whom we may rightfully differ, we should also be asking, What are they doing right? It may be that we will conclude that their emphases may subvert true faith. But in many cases we can also profitably ask, what can we learn from them?[13]

---

[13]Richard F. Lovelace, *Dynamics of Spiritual Life: An Evangelical Theology of Renewal* (Downers Grove, IL: InterVarsity Press, 1979). See especially his sections on proposals for today and unitive evangelicalism, 279-336.

At the same time, we have to recognize that among the bewilderingly diverse churches that the free market has helped shape, there is also lots of room for false teachings that encourage self-deception. It is true that in most types of today's Christianity we can find instances where what C. S. Lewis called "Mere Christianity" or "those beliefs that have been common to all Christians at all times" have survived.[14] So we can cultivate those commonalities and at least recognize that there are widely diverse sorts of mere Christians around the world who are our sisters and brothers. Still the institutional anarchy of Christianity in the modern and postmodern eras also means that such core Christianity is often mixed up with corruptions in teaching or practice that need also to be identified.

Christians today have many views of how to deal with the bewildering variety of church teachings. Jonathan Edwards was a strictly Reformed partisan, and many of his admirers follow him in maintaining that approach to doctrinal and institutional differences. Others are more open to looking for essential commonalities among divergent traditions. We need not try to settle such arguments here. Yet, however such issues are resolved, Edwards, as we shall see, offers every sort of professing Christian some important guidelines for assessing the authenticity of faith.

---

[14]C. S. Lewis, *Mere Christianity*, The Complete C. S. Lewis Signature Classics (New York: HarperOne, 2002), 6.

5

BUT HOW DO WE TELL?
The SIGNS *of* RIGHTLY ORDERED LOVES

EDWARDS SPENT ALMOST his whole life wrestling with the question of how to tell the difference between authentic Christian experience and its imitations: self-delusion and hypocrisy. In his own early years he often struggled in trying to assess the genuineness of his own faith. And as a pastor in a town where people took church membership seriously as a spiritual matter but also held it as a sign of social respectability, he was constantly encountering the question of the authenticity of the professions of his parishioners. Such issues were greatly intensified by the awakenings and their aftermaths. Though he was gratified to see that many of his neighbors and parishioners had been brought to mature faith, he was also deeply disappointed by the falling away of some who had displayed the greatest enthusiasm or been overcome by the deepest emotions.

While Edwards continued to be the chief apologist for the revivalists and had great hopes for the international awakenings that might ensue, he also became deeply concerned about their excesses. As the movement grew, it attracted some evangelists, especially in breakaway groups, who encouraged exhilarating but superficial emotional experiences. Their sensational methods invited self-delusion. Even so, Edwards continued to insist that intense and even overwhelming emotional responses were also often just what one should expect among those who recognize God's grace in their lives. So one had to look beyond the matter of heightened emotions if one was to identify the symptoms of genuine Christian spirituality.

Then, how do you tell? In the mid-1740s, after the Great Awakening had cooled down, Edwards offered his definitive reflections on the answer to that question in one of his masterworks, *A Treatise Concerning Religious Affections*.

After almost three centuries of sometimes anarchical evangelicalism—much of which seems genuinely world-changing, while some seems more superficial and self-serving—it is safe to say that we need Edwards's carefully balanced analysis as much as ever.

For twenty-first-century readers, I think one of the most helpful keys to appreciating Edwards's *Religious Affections* is to translate it as *A Treatise on Religious Loves*. For us, "affections" is not a very compelling word. We tend to think of an affection as a liking or a fondness. People who feel down may seek just a little affection. Sometimes, to be sure, we may speak of deep affections as much stronger experiences, but usually we think of them as moderate feelings or emotions. So when we first hear Edwards say, "True religion consists very much in the affections," our first impression might be that he is merely saying that true religion is not just intellectual but will also involve our feelings and emotions. While it is true that it is not simply intellectual, Edwards is thinking of something deeper than feelings or emotions as his primary meaning when he speaks of religious affections. He begins his account by citing 1 Peter 1:8: "Whom having not seen, ye love; in whom, though now ye see him not, yet believing, ye rejoice with joy unspeakable." The affections he is thinking of are most essentially the sort of *love for a person* that brings joy unspeakable. True affections for Edwards include the joy and delight—at the heart of his theology—of experiencing the beauty of perfect love. The closest human analogy, he suggests, is the joy and delight of a bride and groom for each other.

Yet, as we all know, lots of people who at first were wildly in love have later found that they were misled by their passions and enthusiasm and that the relationship was a huge mistake. Something similar sometimes happens also with once-overwhelming religious experiences. So Edwards is clear that one should set the question of great passions and emotions to the side and concentrate on the question, what are the signs of truly lasting love? What are the traits of those Christians who have a lifetime loving relationship to God?

It is helpful, then, to think of this work for our time as *A Treatise on Religious Loves.* Or if we think back to the Augustinian tradition in which Edwards stands, it could also be called *A Treatise on "Rightly Ordered Religious Loves."* If, by grace, we know God's love, then our lesser loves will reflect that greatest love. So, despite our remaining imperfections, we should be recognizable as those who love what God loves.

———

Edwards begins his treatise with analysis of the centrality of heartfelt loves, or affections, to genuine Christian experiences and then turns to a thorough recounting of those signs that do *not* prove anything one way or the other as to whether one has been truly transformed by the Holy Spirit. These include traits like high emotional experiences, preoccupation with religious things, readiness to quote Scripture, great self-confidence in one's own spirituality, and other traits that can be found among hypocrites as well as among some genuine Christians.

While one of the prominent themes in *Religious Affections* is that heightened, dramatic, and ecstatic emotions in response to the gospel are often misleading and short-lived, Edwards is also careful, as always, to say that they may also be perfectly legitimate. First, it may be entirely appropriate for one who recognizes the grandeur of God's saving grace in their lives to be entirely overwhelmed by emotions. So even people who fall down, scream out, or go into trances might be acting in perfectly appropriate ways and in the long run prove to be mature, balanced Christians.

Edwards had, in fact, a few years before, seen a compelling example of an overwhelming spiritual state in his own wife, Sarah. Early in 1742, while Edwards was away evangelizing in some neighboring towns, Sarah experienced one of the most intense spiritual ecstasies of which we have a detailed record. Following some days of anxiety and depression, she was suddenly transported by the wonderful joy of what she described as a "heavenly Elysium." This euphoric state lasted, in various degrees, for more than two weeks. Sometimes she was so overcome that she would collapse physically, and some of her friends said that they feared she might die before Jonathan got home. Most of the time, however, she simply felt filled with immense spiritual joy, even as she still could go about performing her usual duties overseeing a very large household. When Jonathan returned home, he was delighted to learn of his Sarah's wonderful ecstasies, and he carefully recorded her account. In a subsequent treatise defending the awakenings, he used this account, disguising the source, as evidence that even overwhelming, extravagant religious experiences might be entirely appropriate responses to experiencing God's amazing grace. Knowing Sarah (as he did) as an admired spiritual model, he could write that this was not the deceiving enthusiasm of a recent convert. Rather, these were appropriate raptures of a saint of proven and longstanding maturity. And, in answer to those who might say that such extreme emotions might be a sign of mental instability, Edwards affirmed: "If such things are . . . the fruit of a distempered brain, let my brain be evermore possessed of that happy distemper."[1]

Yet Edwards also knew well how self-deceptive strong emotions could be. He had seen that especially clearly from observing his parishioners in Northampton after each of the awakenings there. Once the ardors of the awakening had cooled, some of the most enthusiastic, whom he had thought were genuinely converted, reverted to their old ways. So he includes in *Religious Affections* a long section on signs that are not reliable

---

[1] Jonathan Edwards, "Some Thoughts Concerning the Present Revival of Religion in New England," in *The Great Awakening*, ed. C. C. Goen, vol. 4 in *The Works of Jonathan Edwards* (New Haven, CT: Yale University Press, 1972), 341. The twenty-six-volume series is hereafter in this chapter referred to as *WJE* with volume number and page.

evidences of true religion. And throughout the treatise he keeps pointing out the dangers of self-deception and superficial piety. Still, Edwards never abandons his stance that if people truly experience the marvelous, life-changing work of the Holy Spirit, then sometimes the most extravagant emotional responses are entirely appropriate.

Having cleared away the signs that are not reliable evidences of genuine Christian faith, Edwards turns to the heart of his treatise and the part that provides the valuable insights for today. These are found in his concluding exposition of twelve "positive signs" of genuine spirituality. In presenting these traits of genuine Christian experience, Edwards is very careful to say that there are no absolutely definitive tests. Our human capabilities for self-deceit are too great for that. So there is no simple checklist that, once completed, allows us to rest assured in our genuine spiritual state. Rather, whether in looking at others or ourselves, we have to recognize the limits of our vision. As Edwards puts it: "A fixed star is easily distinguishable from a comet, in a clear sky; but if we view them through a cloud, it may be impossible to see the difference."[2] Even for true believers, the remaining presence of sin clouds their vision. There are passages in Scripture that speak of gaining assurance of one's faith, such as 1 Corinthians 9:26, where the apostle Paul says, "I therefore so run, not as uncertainly." But, observes Edwards in a critique of armchair or academic Christians, "He obtained assurance of winning the prize, more by running, than by considering."[3] Also, the self-satisfied sinfulness of those who are hypocrites or who

---

[2]Jonathan Edwards, *Religious Affections*, ed. John E. Smith, *WJE* 2:194-95.
[3]Edwards, *Religious Affections*, *WJE* 2:196.

have been deluded will blind them to recognizing their true estate.

Still, even as he acknowledges the limits of his project, Edwards's exposition of the twelve positive signs offers us an immensely valuable analysis of what are the best evidences of true religious experience. Even though we must always recognize that the clouds of our sin and self-regard may be blinding us, these signs nonetheless provide a set of ideals that should be the goals for each of us if we are to truly "press toward the mark" (Philippians 3:14).

To understand Edwards's way of identifying these symptoms of rightly ordered loves, it will also be helpful to go back and be reminded of the classic Christian story of sin and salvation that provides his basic framework. Humans were originally created with a capacity to properly subordinate their self-love to love of God and of what God loves and commands. Adam and Eve, however, rebelled against God's loving rule, loving more to follow their own desires. Being rebels, they were cast out of the Garden of Eden and incurred the guilt for their sin. Moreover, their nature, and hence human nature, was corrupted, so that self-love naturally reigns in every human and will continue to do so unless checked.[4] There is, however, a solution: "As in Adam all die, even so in Christ shall all be made alive" (1 Corinthians 15:22).

The transforming grace that sinners receive results in having their eyes opened to perceive the perfect love manifested in Christ's sacrifice on the cross for their sins. Truly recognizing

---

[4]Edwards, along with other strict Calvinists, held that the guilt of Adam and Eve's sin was imputed to the entire human race.

the beauty of that love will bring a response of love in return. Such true love will then dominate one's life. So one should be able to say that Christ lives in me as Lord. But Christ's rule as Lord should not be some burdensome thing that we have to put up with and submit to. Rather, as in other totally loving commitments, as to a spouse, child, parent, or close friend, we will gladly respond to that love by acting lovingly in return.

Even for those who have been so transformed by God's grace, the problem remains that humans persist in being flawed by their own selfishness. Even when we love Christ, our self-love remains. A degree of self-love is inevitable and appropriate. Yet we must be especially careful that it be kept in its proper place. As Edwards explains in a helpful analogy, self-love is "like fire in an house: which, we say, is a good servant, but a bad master; very useful while kept in its place, but if left to take possession of the whole house, so brings all to destruction."[5]

Even the most faithful Christians always must be on guard not to let those misplaced fires, or loves, take over. They constantly have to take care that the sparks of their passions and desires are not flying out and taking control.

Often, though, the challenge is more subtle than the analogy of a house fire might suggest. It is easy enough to identify our condition if our life is going down in flames due to uncontrolled passions. Yet, for those who have a degree of discipline, the persistence of the dominance of self-love may be more difficult to identify. Once again we need to be reminded that humans have a great capacity for self-deception, to believe what they want to believe, and particularly to think too highly of

---

[5]Jonathan Edwards, *Original Sin*, ed. Clyde A. Holbrook, *WJE* 3:382-83.

themselves. Confirmation bias is an age-old problem. That is, we tend to accept only the evidence that confirms what we already believe and to ignore all evidence to the contrary. Such biases are nowhere more dominant than in our view of our self. So when it comes to religious commitment, people can easily fool themselves as well as others. Particularly respectable people, whose lives are more or less in order and have some desire to be Christian, may convince themselves that they are indeed following Christ. In fact, their love of self may be their dominant love and their "love" of Christ is actually serving that higher love. They might not be consciously hypocritical but just really good at fooling themselves. And testing whether that is the case is even more difficult because of the persistence of sin in true believers.

Given, then, the perversity of the human condition that clouds our vision, what are the best evidences to look for to distinguish genuine Christian faith and rightly ordered loves from the counterfeits?

———

Not surprisingly, Edwards's starting point for those who are looking for the signs of genuine Christian loves is another version of his main themes in "A Divine and Supernatural Light." True religious love, he emphasizes, is a relationship to God in which the Holy Spirit dwells in the Christian as "a new vital principle." The recipient of the grace of this wonderful personal relationship will have a "new sense" of God's love that the unconverted might know about theoretically but not experience. Through "the saving influences of the Spirit of God, there is a new inward perception in their minds, entirely different in its nature and kind, from anything that ever their minds were the subjects to before they were sanctified." Once again, as in the sermon, he uses the analogy that the person who experiences the redemptive love of God in Christ is like the person who has experienced the taste of honey. Others may know theoretically that honey is sweet, but they will never truly know that sweetness until they taste it. Or, he says, the difference between the experience of encountering the love of Christ and just knowing about it is like the difference between those who can actually see colors and the person born blind, who can only hear about them. One must be given eyes to see.[6]

Such a new sense of divine love is then something those who remain in their natural state of ruling self-love can never fully experience. They may have some intense religious experiences that they find exhilarating. And they may be eager to have such emotional highs again. But they are ultimately seeking self-satisfaction rather than experiencing the life-reorienting change of a new higher personal relationship and love.

Such a true sense of the love of God is not only a high standard, but a "sense" has a subjective dimension. In other words, those who have never had it might mistake its imitations for the real thing. Given our capacity for self-deceit, there is no foolproof test. Still, in the second and third signs that Edwards identifies, he offers some other crucial symptoms to look for. The second of these signs is that we should be able to find that our love is truly centered on the one we love rather than on any self-love that is calculating what we will get

---

[6]Edwards, *Religious Affections*, WJE 2:205-6.

out of it. And the third sign is closely related: one should have "a love to divine things for the beauty and sweetness of their moral excellency."[7] And what is "the beauty and sweetness of their moral excellency"? It is preeminently the beauty of love itself, or the beauty of rightly ordered personal relationships. That is the highest, and in Edwards's terms, the sweetest, sort of beauty that we experience. That beauty of rightly ordered loving relationships is like the beauty of flowers in a garden that need the sunlight: ultimately they depend on the light of the highest beauty, the beauty of the loving triune God. As the flowers are drawn to the sunlight, so the true child of God will be drawn to the moral beauties of the Creator, Redeemer, and Comforter. We come back, then, to a central theme in Edwards's theology: if we recognize the love that emanates from the person of the triune God, we will be drawn into the circle of that love as the ultimate sustenance of our life. We can see that love displayed most poignantly in the sacrificial love of Christ, an immensely costly and compassionate love directed toward rebellious creatures who do not deserve it. Since we are all born as essentially self-centered rebels against God, perceiving the beauty of Christ's sacrificial love must involve the work of the Holy Spirit, giving us eyes to see. So if we are truly living in the light of Christ's love, we should be able to recognize the signs in our lives that we are truly enthralled by the beauty of Christ's love and so are drawn to it and think of how we should love in return.

Of course, even in such inquiries, some may deceive themselves and be loving only what they get out of it. And for true

---

[7]Edwards, *Religious Affections*, WJE 2:254.

believers the issue is complicated by the fact that they *do* get something out of it. The principle is "seek ye first the kingdom of God . . . and all these things shall be added unto you" (Matthew 6:33). But we can all too easily think that we love serving God when what we really love is our pleasure in thinking that we are serving God. Our highest desire should be to be drawn into the orbit of Christ's love, so that we love what Christ loves. Yet even the best of believers often loses sight of the beauty of the moral excellency of that love and becomes preoccupied with love to self and other lesser loves.

One practical way to think about it is to ask how central God is to our picture of reality: if God is anywhere in our picture of reality, then surely God has to be in the center of that picture. Our natural inclination is always to see ourselves at the center of things and everyone and everything else, including God, as on the periphery. We may pray to God about lots of things, but too often we are asking help for furthering self-centered desires or goals. God can too easily become a background figure whom we treat as providing a sort of cosmic insurance policy. Since it is easy even for Christians to lapse into such attitudes, we need constantly to be reminded to recognize that God is at the center of reality. And we should recognize that, despite our ever-present sense that we alone are at the center, in reality we are on the periphery, just like everyone else. That is the radical reorientation of what we recognize as the epicenter of our world, and reminding ourselves of it requires the ongoing work of the Holy Spirit. If we have the grace to try to cultivate such an outlook, then it should begin to change the way we perceive everything, what we love, and what we do.

Such a reorientation of our loves, Edwards is saying, is possible only if we enter into a loving relationship with the perfectly loving God. In a loving relationship, one's love of self does not disappear but is reshaped by the love of another for whom one would even sacrifice one's life if necessary. When we are drawn to the beauty of God, who first loved us, then we are entering into a relationship that will reshape our other loves, including love of self.

Edwards goes on in his fourth sign to further elaborate the all-important foundational principle that the true believer has a new spiritual sense. That new sense is not just a feeling. "Holy affections are not heat without light."[8] They involve a new *quality* of apprehension and appreciation of God and divine things that the unregenerate person lacks. It is "a sense of the heart, of the supreme beauty and sweetness of holiness or moral perfection of divine things."[9] It is an ability to appreciate "true moral beauty."[10] His most helpful analogies are to how one might appreciate other sorts of beauty. A person who relishes the external beauties of nature does not need to reason about the proportions and relationships of what he sees to recognize true beauty. Or in recognizing the beauty of the countenance of someone we love, it does not take any reasoning, but it takes "only the glance of an eye." Musical appreciation provides helpful analogies. It is something like the difference between a person who not only appreciates, but thrills to great music and someone who find it tedious. "He who has a rectified musical ear," says Edwards, "knows whether the sound he hears be true harmony:

---

[8]Edwards, *Religious Affections*, WJE 2:266.
[9]Edwards, *Religious Affections*, WJE 2:272.
[10]Edwards, *Religious Affections*, WJE 2:281.

he doesn't need first to be at the trouble of the reasonings of a mathematician, about the proportion of the notes."[11] The difference between such a person's appreciation of great music and knowledge about that music and someone who is not enthralled by its beauty is analogous to the difference between the true believer's appreciation and love of divine things and the merely intellectual knowledge about them that the unregenerate person may have.[12]

Having emphasized that qualitative difference in ways of knowing, Edwards is careful to specify in his fifth sign that, even though one's loves are the heart of true religious experience, right understanding is also involved. That understanding needs to be informed by Scripture. So our religious beliefs and experiences are not to be based on visions or dreams, ecstatic experiences or strong impressions that God is speaking to us. And at the same time, Edwards makes a point of saying that we cannot demand of ordinary believers an extensive theological understanding as a necessary condition for true faith. Many children or people of very limited understanding may nonetheless truly know the love of God in Christ.

A central feature in Edwards's analysis, explored in the sixth sign, is that true Christians should be characterized by *humility*. Edwards highlights humility as "a great and most essential thing in true religion."[13] In that emphasis, he stands firmly in the Augustinian and Reformed tradition—and in fact in a note he quotes John Calvin, who in turn quotes Augustine, saying that if asked what was the first precept of the Christian religion,

---

[11]Edwards, *Religious Affections*, WJE 2:281.
[12]Edwards, *Religious Affections*, WJE 2:271, 282.
[13]Edwards, *Religious Affections*, WJE 2:312.

"I would answer, firstly, humility, secondly, and thirdly, and forever, humility."[14]

Emphasizing humility before God as a major characteristic to look for in the Christian's life is the counterpart to Edwards's earlier point that the principal characteristic of hypocrites is that they are in love with their religious experience; they value it for what they get out of it. In his sermon series on *Charity and Its Fruits,* Edwards says that one characteristic of the person who is humble before God is that he "is not disposed to trust in himself."[15] That might seem like a very conventional religious principle. But if we think about it in the American context, as we considered the dominant heritage in the tradition of Franklin, then it goes very much against the grain of the attitudes that are so much celebrated in our culture. We might think of Ralph Waldo Emerson as another early prophet of the American creed. In his famous essay "Self-Reliance," Emerson affirms exactly the opposite of Edwards and the larger Christian heritage: "Trust thyself. Every heart vibrates to that iron string."[16] Though Emerson was an elite pundit, what he said resonates with many of the popular American sentiments as well, both elite on the left and populist on the right. Much of American religion, including both the liberal Protestant tradition and many populist evangelical varieties, has been about Christianity as essentially self-fulfillment, being free from restraints, and being true to oneself.

I once heard a sermon by a liberal preacher who invented the testimony of the apostle Philip to make his point. Unlike others

---

[14]Edwards, *Religious Affections,* WJE 2:314-15.

[15]Edwards, "Charity and Its Fruits," in *Ethical Writings,* WJE 8:239.

[16]Emerson, "Self-Reliance" (1841), in *The Annotated Emerson,* ed. David Mikics and Phillip Lopate (Cambridge, MA: Harvard University Press, 2012), 162.

of the apostles, we hear little of Philip after the Gospel accounts. According to the preacher, Philip explained this by saying that Jesus meant many different things to different people. "When he looked you in the eye he was saying, 'Be yourself, Philip, just be yourself.'" In contrast to some others of the apostles, who were activists and got themselves martyred, or Thomas, who went the whole way to India, Philip stayed home and tended his own garden. The gospel of Philip was, in effect, the good news that he should just be Philip!

Classic Christianity, by way of contrast, preaches self-renunciation and humility. And in the midst of the sometimes tumultuous early evangelical awakenings, Edwards himself was particularly concerned with how the evangelical emphasis on conversion can lead to a false humility. He was especially aware of the Catch-22 that people who think they have given up self for Christ may soon be taking pride in having achieved the humility of self-renunciation. So Edwards says, "An infallible sign of spiritual pride is persons being apt to think highly of their humility." As Edwards had seen after years of promoting awakenings, false humility becomes especially likely when people's religious emotions are raised to great intensity, and we know that was one of his chief concerns in counseling. We learn that from a letter of advice that he wrote to a teenage convert, Deborah Hathaway, at the height of the awakenings in 1741. He advises:

> Remember, that pride is the worst viper that is in the heart, the greatest disturber of the soul's peace, and of sweet communion with Christ: it was the first sin committed, and lies lowest in the foundation of Satan's whole building, and is

with the greatest difficulty rooted out, and is the most hidden, secret, and deceitful of all lusts, and often creeps insensibly into the midst of religion, even, sometimes, under the disguise of humility itself.

He goes on to emphasize to Deborah that the true Christian must be "like a child" who is taking the hand of Jesus rather than thinking oneself better than others.[17]

———

After reiterating in his seventh sign that true believers have undergone "a change of nature,"[18] which is the transformation that underlies all the other signs, Edwards concludes with five signs that can be seen as a portrait of what a truly humble child of Christ should look like. With this portrayal Edwards provides his readers with a sort of template to help see what we should expect to find in a genuine Christian. Though our residual, old, selfish natures may keep getting in the way, we can see from this sketch the traits of the beauty of rightly ordered loves.

The first of these traits (the eighth sign) is particularly striking today. Those who have received a new nature should be characterized by "the lamblike, dovelike spirit and temper of Jesus Christ." These lamblike, dovelike qualities, he explains, "naturally beget and promote such a spirit of love, meekness, quietness, forgiveness and mercy, as appeared in Christ."[19] Being characterized by such qualities, he affirms, is nothing less than a fundamental of the faith. If the Bible is to be trusted, he insists

---

[17]Jonathan Edwards to Deborah Hathaway, June 3, 1741, in *Letters and Personal Writings*, ed. George S. Claghorn, *WJE* 16:94.

[18]Edwards, *Religious Affections*, *WJE* 2:340.

[19]Edwards, *Religious Affections*, *WJE* 2:344-45.

with great conviction, then one who lacks these qualities cannot be a true Christian.

Edwards's uncompromising firmness on this point is particularly needed today because it is so seldom emphasized, let alone insisted on, in much of recent evangelicalism. Particularly in the United States, when people speak of evangelical Christians, these are rarely the qualities that come to mind. Not that these biblical teachings are missing altogether, but the radically gentle and pacific implications of being given a new nature are rarely emphasized, as they are by Edwards, as essential marks of true Christians. Sometimes teachings concerning cultivating these Christlike qualities may be familiar themes in more liberal churches where the gospel has been limited largely to therapeutic and sentimental themes. In most evangelical churches, by way of contrast, we seldom hear of such emphases as among the fundamental implications of being "born again."[20]

In recent generations one prominent characteristic of a good many American evangelicals is to emphasize the bold, manly, and militant aspects of the faith. Evangelicalism around the world, and in America also, comes in countless varieties, so there are always exceptions to any generalization. Yet much of American evangelicalism has an earlier heritage in the fundamentalist movement of a century ago, when warfare furnished prominent imagery in their campaigns against religious modernism and secularizing culture. Such emphases on embattlement

---

[20]Given the many varieties of evangelicals, there have been and still are some notable exceptions. Particularly, churches that emphasize personal holiness may stress these qualities, as churches in the Anabaptist tradition often do. In most other evangelical traditions, such teachings have often been subordinated to other concerns rather than being stressed as essential.

persist in a good many evangelical churches. And in the past half century, explicit emphases on "biblical manhood" have become especially prominent. One subgroup among whom such emphases were especially, sometimes notoriously, conspicuous in the early twenty-first century was the renewal movement among Reformed churches, then characterized as young, restless, and Reformed.[21] That is especially ironic, since that same movement also promoted a high regard for Jonathan Edwards. Yet some of those who have most celebrated Edwards have also celebrated manly militancy in ways that are contrary to what Edwards sees as one of the fundamental qualities of a genuine child of Christ.

Since these issues remain a matter of much current debate, we can look especially closely at Edwards's remarkable emphasis on "the lamblike, dovelike spirit and temper of Jesus Christ" as a fundamental Christian trait.

Edwards himself often encountered those who used their Christian profession for self-aggrandizement, self-assertion, or to diminish and disparage others. At least that is what we can surmise from the great passion with which Edwards writes about the necessity of Christians manifesting the "lamblike" and "dovelike" qualities of Jesus. He goes on for more than twenty pages, mostly demonstrating that the biblical emphasis on this point is so "very abundant," as to put beyond dispute that such traits are essential marks of any true Christians.[22] At the heart of

---

[21]Collin Hansen, *Young, Restless, Reformed: A Journalist's Journey with the New Calvinists* (Wheaton, IL: Crossway, 2008). See also Kristin Kobes Du Mez, *Jesus and John Wayne: How White Evangelicals Corrupted a Faith and Fractured a Nation* (New York: W. W. Norton, 2020), for a sharp critique of the role of masculinity in this and other American evangelical movements.

[22]Edwards, *Religious Affections, WJE* 2:345.

the gospel are the radical teachings of Jesus in the Sermon on the Mount, that blessedness is to be found in the meek, the merciful, and in those who become like little children. Likewise, the apostle Paul repeatedly exhorts the elect to such virtues, as in Colossians 3:12-13, where he urges "mercies, kindness, humbleness of mind, meekness, longsuffering; forbearing . . . and forgiving." Or in 1 Corinthians 13, similar traits of humbleness and deference to others are among the traits of true charity. Or the "fruit of the Spirit" in Galatians 5 include "love, joy, peace, longsuffering, gentleness, goodness, faith, meekness, temperance."[23] These are just some of the best-known biblical highlights, but Edwards offers page after page of Scripture texts showing that these are not only characteristic of Christ but should be most evident in any who are in Christ.

Edwards anticipates that some will object that there is also a place for "Christian fortitude and the boldness for Christ, being good soldiers in the Christian warfare, and in coming out boldly against the enemies of Christ and his people." There indeed is, he concedes, a place for fortitude and boldness in literal warfare "against those endeavoring to overthrow the kingdom of Christ and the interest of religion." But he immediately adds that "many people seem to be quite mistaken about the nature of Christian fortitude," who would make the attitudes of the brutal fierceness of human warfare a model for Christian attitudes more generally. "Though Christian fortitude appears, in withstanding and counteracting the enemies that are without us," he acknowledges, "yet it much more appears, in resisting and suppressing the enemies that are within us." These are the enemies of pride

---

[23]Edwards, *Religious Affections*, *WJE* 2:345-46.

and self-aggrandizement that are the opposites of "meekness, sweetness, and benevolence of mind." As Proverbs 16:32 says, "He that is slow to anger is better than the mighty; and he that ruleth his spirit than he that taketh a city."[24]

And when we think of Christian warfare as one of the metaphors that should shape the Christian's life, we also should think of our captain, Jesus Christ, as the model for conducting such warfare. He could have resisted his oppressors with the fierceness of a roaring lion. But he instead showed his valor as a gentle lamb. So if we are to follow Christ in boldness and valor, it should not be

in the exercise of any fiery passions; not in fierce and violent speeches, and vehemently declaiming against, and of crying out of the intolerable wickedness of the opposers, giving 'em their own plain terms; but in not opening his mouth when afflicted and oppressed, in going as a lamb to the slaughter, and as a sheep before his shearers, is dumb; not opening his mouth; praying that the father will forgive his cruel enemies, because they knew not what they did.[25]

Edwards concedes that some true Christians may have a difficult temperament and the remains of a contrary spirit, so that they sometimes act in ways inconsistent with Christ's lamblike, forgiving nature. Yet Edwards insists that there are no true Christians who are not dominated by these Christlike traits. "But this I affirm," he declares,

and shall affirm till I deny the Bible to be worth anything, that everything in Christians that belongs to true Christianity

---

[24]All quotations in this paragraph are from Edwards, *Religious Affections*, WJE 2:350.
[25]Edwards, *Religious Affections*, WJE 2:351.

is of this tendency and works this way: and that there is no true Christian on earth, but is so under the prevailing power of such a spirit, that he is properly denominated by it, and it is truly and justly his character.[26]

––––––––

Edwards continues with the theme of gentleness in the next (the ninth) sign, which he summarizes as "Gracious Affections soften the heart, and are attended and followed with a Christian tenderness of spirit."[27] His point is a more familiar one than the previous one and requires less summary—not that its familiarity makes it any less important.

When he says that genuine affections "soften the heart," he means that they produce the opposite of what the Bible means when it says that characters like Pharaoh had a "hardened heart" when told by God to let his people go. Persons of soft hearts or "tenderness of spirit" will be open to obeying the will of God. They will not reserve a place for the dominance of their own will and the preservation of a realm of sin in some areas of their life, even while conforming to Christian principles in other ways. Rather, their hearts will be open to seeking and loving God's will. Once again, as in the previous sign, the opposite of "tenderness of spirit" is pride. Hardness of heart is pride that has established a fortress where the self continues to reign, even while professing

––––––––

[26]Edwards, *Religious Affections*, WJE 2:356. Even in cases where a person's natural temperament is bold and fierce, Edwards maintains that if conversion is genuine, it will mean that that lamblike and meek peacemaking qualities of Christ will become dominant. Some converts, he remarks, may have formerly been like wolves and serpents, but the gospel is supposed to overcome other powerful vices such as drunkenness and lasciviousness. Edwards, *Religious Affections*, WJE 2:357.

[27]Edwards, *Religious Affections*, WJE 2:357.

to truly follow Christ and his will. Once again, Edwards invokes one of his favorite images, that of becoming like a little child. (Jonathan and Sarah had eleven children, and Jonathan himself had ten siblings, including five younger sisters, we might be reminded.) A little child that is of a tender heart can easily be won by kindness and will weep with those that weep and fear what is fearful.[28] Such a child will readily turn to a loving parent and trust the parent for guidance. So likewise the true Christian's heart will be open to following God's will, avoiding what God forbids, and loving what God loves.

Edwards explicitly suggests his ideal that true Christians should be beautiful people in his tenth sign, that true affections will differ from false in that they will manifest "beautiful symmetry and proportion." He immediately goes on to acknowledge that true Christians often show poor proportion in their lives due to bad judgments, defects in temperament, imperfections of grace, lack of education, poor instruction, and many other reasons. But whatever failings they may have will be far less than the "monstrous disproportions" of affections seen in false religion, hypocrites, and counterfeit saints.[29]

Edwards's standard for beauty, it should be recalled, reflected eighteenth-century ideals of beauty as found in harmonious proportions. The grandeur of the music of J. S. Bach might be the best example. Edwards also sees beautiful symmetries that are not formal. So in some of his meditations he speaks glowingly of beautiful symmetry and proportions in nature, as in the complex mixture of lights, colors, shapes, flowers, and trees on

---

[28]Edwards, *Religious Affections*, WJE 2:361.
[29]Edwards, *Religious Affections*, WJE 2:365.

a beautiful day, which have an indefinable beauty and harmony.[30] Once again, we can be reminded that he sees such beauties in God's creation as images and shadows of the higher beauties of harmonies among persons in properly loving relationships. And ultimately these point to the highest beauty—that is, the sacrificial, weeping love of Christ that should orient our other loves.

Despite the residual imperfections and limitations of all Christians, then, we should expect to see some manifestations of the beauty of properly ordered loves in anyone who is truly redeemed. For instance, says Edwards, in illustrating the balanced Christian life, great rejoicing in forgiveness from sins should have its counterpart in continuing sorrow for sins. Or those who broadly proclaim their love and benevolence should not in fact be more often characterized by their "contention, envy, revenge, evil-speaking," and so forth. And they should not have "flowing affections" toward some people but be "full of bitterness toward others." Some who show great love to those of their own party hate those of the opposite faction. Or they might show great love and benevolence to their immediate neighbors but not to strangers. Others might love fellow church members but disdain the sinners outside of the faith. Or some might care for the welfare of their neighbors' bodies but not for their souls. Among the most common traits of hypocrites is that they will make a great show of rejoicing in what God has done for them while neglecting basic Christian duties—or, as Edwards often encountered to his great regret, their zeal for religion is raised for a time, but then, like a comet, disappears.[31]

---

[30]Miscellany 108, in *Miscellanies a–500, WJE* 13:279.
[31]Edwards, *Religious Affections, WJE* 2:365-76. Quotations from 368.

Edwards's reflections on the properly balanced life of the mature Christian suggest a way for us to consider whether our loves are properly ordered. We can take a sort of personal inventory to ask whether, despite apparent signs of grace in a few areas of our lives, there might not be other areas that we are neglecting. We need regularly to be reminded that living in harmony with God and loving what God loves should help shape the full range of our attitudes, commitments, convictions, character traits, and practices. And as his examples suggest, it is easy to let our zeal for one aspect of the faith blind us to what should be equally important concerns.

Edwards adds, in his eleventh sign, a fairly simple test for identifying genuine converts in contrast to those who would shine brightly with enthusiasm during an awakening, but after a time their fervor would fade. Among those who truly love God, "the higher [their affections] are raised, the more a spiritual appetite and longing of the soul after spiritual attainments" is increased. "On the contrary, false affections rest satisfied in themselves."[32] Superficial religious experience is ultimately oriented toward satisfying oneself rather than satisfying God. One of the most common forms of self-deception that he observed was that of those who fell in love with their own ecstatic religious experiences. They are like teenagers who are in love with being in love. Love becomes an end in itself.

Edwards quotes the Puritan author Thomas Shepard as saying, "An hypocrite's last end is to satisfy himself: hence he has enough. A saint's is to satisfy Christ: but never has enough."[33] Edwards

---

[32]Edwards, *Religious Affections*, WJE 2:376.
[33]Edwards, *Religious Affections*, WJE 2:380n, citing Thomas Shepard, *Parable of the Ten Virgins*, pt. I (London, 1660), 157.

underscores the point, remarking that "the Scriptures everywhere represent the seeking, striving and labor of a Christian, as being chiefly after his conversion, and his conversion as being but the beginning of his work."[34]

————

Edwards culminates his portrait of a genuine Christian by highlighting the crowning evidence that is the surest test of true affections: action. His arguments for this point go on for seventy-eight pages, while he averages about seventeen pages for each of the other eleven. He dwells on this theme because it is so fundamental to any true understanding of Christianity. Our affections or loves are what shape our actions. So if we truly love God, it will be evident in what we do. To truly love God is to be drawn to the "excellency of divine things"—that is, "their moral excellency or beauty of their holiness." Those who see that beauty will "delight" in it and desire "to be adorned" with it. And what they delight in, they will be inspired to do.[35] So those who see the beauty of God's love in Christ will desire to be conformed to that beauty. They will be drawn to love what God loves, and those loves will shape their actions. In their unperfected state, true Christians will, of course, sometimes lapse from those practices and will, in sins of omission, fail to do all that they should. But one sign of true Christians who are drawn to the beauty of God's love is that their desire will always be to do better and to be more attuned to God's will, seeking to *grow* in grace. And that seeking will not be out of

————

[34]Edwards, *Religious Affections*, WJE 2:381-82.
[35]Edwards, *Religious Affections*, WJE 2:394.

grudging duty but rather like the seeking for how to better show one's love to one's beloved.

Even though the good deeds of Christians are the preeminent sign of grace, those good works, of course, are not the ground of grace.[36] One's salvation depends not on what we do but rather on God first opening our eyes to see God's perfect beauty and love and so to reorient our love and our actions. Rather than loving self above all things, we begin to love God above all things. Our good works will be the result, but not the cause, of that transformation.

Edwards employs all his argumentative skills in this culminating section of *Religious Affections*. This point is so essential to him that he goes to immense lengths to prove his basic thesis— that gracious affections have their fruit in practice—from an abundance of scriptural passages and from reason.

Fortunately, since Edwards often preached on such themes, we can find more pastoral presentations of such emphases in some of his sermons. Frankly, Edwards in his most argumentative mode, as he is in this last section of *Religious Affections*, can be painfully thorough. So it will be easier to see the practical meaning of these essential teachings from how he presented them to his congregations.

The easiest place to find Edwards's more pastoral versions of such advice is in his well-known sermon series *Charity and Its Fruits*. Those twelve sermons are expositions of the lyrical passage on Christian love ("charity" in the King James Version) in 1 Corinthians 13. So, for instance, in the tenth sermon, "Grace Tends to Holy Practice," Edwards makes the same essential

---

[36]Cf., Paul Ramsey, introduction to *Ethical Writings*, by Jonathan Edwards, ed. Paul Ramsey, *WJE* 8:40.

points as in the culmination of *Religious Affections* but in a much more practical way:

> Are you sensible of the beauty and pleasantness of ways of holy practice? Do you see the beauty of holiness, the loveliness of the ways of God and Christ? It is said in the text, that charity rejoiceth in the truth; and that is given as the character of the godly that he rejoices and works righteousness, *Isaiah 64:5*. And how often does the Psalmist speak of the law of God as being his delight, and how he loves God's commandments [*Psalm 1:2* and *Psalm 119:6*]! [37]

In the sermons of *Charity and Its Fruits*, as in *Religious Affections*, the beauty of genuine faith will be most evident in acts of love to neighbor. As he puts it in the sermon on "Holy Practice":

> "Hereby we know that we are of the truth." No other love to brethren but that which shows itself in deeds of love will profit any man. *James 2:15-16*, "If a brother or sister be naked, and destitute of daily food, and one of you say unto them, Depart in peace, be ye warmed and filled; notwithstanding ye give them not those things which are needful to the body; what doth it profit?" Experience shows that those for whom men have a sincere love, they are ready both to do and to suffer for. [38]

Ronald Story's book *Jonathan Edwards and the Gospel of Love* provides an especially helpful account of Edwards's continued emphasis on the duty of those who were rich to care for the poor. As a young pastor, Edwards recognized that as one of his greatest

---

[37] Edwards, "Charity and Its Fruits," in *Ethical Writings*, WJE 8:310.
[38] Edwards, "Charity and Its Fruits," in *Ethical Writings*, WJE 8:307.

practical challenges in his parish. Despite the longstanding presence of the church, Northampton was a cantankerous small town. It was on the western frontier, where life was often hard, and the people were given to competitiveness and petty jealousies, often lacking a communal spirit. That was especially evident in the attitude of the rich toward the poor. Given some great disparities in wealth, Edwards recommended that the rich should give 25 percent of their wealth to the poor, as he heard was done by some Pietists in Germany. Eventually he also succeeded in enlisting the town government to join with church deacons in establishing a welfare fund.[39]

Early in his pastoral ministry, Edwards emphasized how deeply he was committed to such social concerns in a four-part sermon preached in 1733, "The Duty of Charity to the Poor." Preaching on Deuteronomy 15:7-11, he made clear that such charity was not some sort of optional add-on for Christians but (as he put it in stating the "doctrine" of this sermon): "*'Tis the most absolute and indispensable duty of a people of God to give bountifully and willingly for the supply of the wants of the needy.*" He goes on to underscore the point by asking rhetorically, "Where have we any command in the Bible laid down in stronger terms, and in a more preemptory urgent manner than the command of giving to the poor?" And in case anyone missed it, he reiterates in broader terms, "And I know of scarce any particular duty that is so much insisted upon, so pressed and urged

---

[39]Ronald Story, *Jonathan Edwards and the Gospel of Love* (Amherst: University of Massachusetts Press, 2012), 63 and passim. See also Gerald McDermott and Ronald Story, *The Other Jonathan Edwards: Selected Writings on Society, Love, and Justice* (Amherst: University of Massachusetts Press, 2015), which includes many of Edwards's sermons on this topic.

upon us, both in the Old Testament and New, as the duty of charity to the poor."[40]

Edwards underscores the point further by citing a host of texts from both Old and New Testament, making the point that this theme is central to all of Scripture, culminating in the message of Christ himself, who "for your sakes . . . became poor" (2 Corinthians 8:9). "Mercy" is one of the "weightier matters of the law" that the Pharisees and the self-righteous legalists of the church most often neglected. And most decisively, Jesus in Matthew 25 depicts the last judgment as a time when the sheep and the goats are separated precisely on the basis of what they have done for the needy, culminating with "inasmuch as ye have done it unto one of the least of these my brethren, ye have done it unto me" (Matthew 25:40).[41]

Edwards points out that "what you have is not your own, i.e., you have no absolute right to it, have only a subordinate right." We are merely stewards of our possessions, and we will have to answer to God as to how we have used them. So releasing our hold on the material things over which we have been given charge is the sort of evidence of subordinating self-love to love of God that we should expect to see in true Christians. Yet, since recognition that we are not our own restores us to our proper relation to God, it is ultimately also in our highest self-interest. Hence Edwards points out that the Scriptures are filled with promises as to the benefits of giving to the needy. "Blessed are the merciful: for they shall obtain mercy" (Matthew 5:7). We are laying up treasures in heaven (see Luke 12:33). Giving to the poor

---

[40]Jonathan Edwards, "The Duty of Charity to the Poor," in *Sermons and Discourses, 1730–1733*, ed. Mark Valeri, *WJE* 17:373-75. Italics in original.

[41]Edwards, "The Duty of Charity to the Poor," *WJE* 17:379-82.

is like lending to God with the promise we will be more than well repaid. Or it is like sowing seed for a crop, something we give up only temporarily but will be richly rewarded. Those who sow "bountifully shall reap also bountifully" (2 Corinthians 9:6).[42]

Having pointed to the preeminence of charity among the Christian's duties, Edwards turns in his sermon to answer the many common excuses rich Christians use to avoid these biblical commands. One objection is that the poor neighbor is a person of "ill temper" who has done harm to us and does not deserve our charity. Edwards cites the parable of the Good Samaritan to show how Christ teaches us who is our neighbor. We are also told that we must forgive those who trespass against us. We are commanded to love even our enemies, remembering that Christ died for us even though we are undeserving. And to the common objection that they have "nothing to spare," Edwards replies that what people really mean is that they cannot give to the poor without some degree of inconvenience to their own lifestyle. Yet, once again, we must be reminded that Christ made himself poor and truly suffered for our sakes.

To the objection is that it is "their own fault" that some persons are in need, Edwards points out that sometimes people lack the natural faculties to manage their affairs. And even when some do not correct their ways, we should still be giving to relieve their innocent family members who may suffer from that person's faults. Or, if we object that we cannot tell whether some persons are proper objects of charity or whether they will simply misuse our gift, Edwards offers a clinching argument that needs to be heard as a principle of charity in every era: "'tis better to

---

[42]Edwards, "The Duty of Charity to the Poor," *WJE* 17:379-85.

give to several that are not objects of charity, than to send away empty one that is."[43]

Timothy Keller well summarizes this same biblical message for today:

> How do you know you've really been born again? You care about the poor. When you see people without resources, your heart goes out to them. If it doesn't, maybe you're saved, but you're lacking the evidence of salvation. Justification leads to justice. Justice is the sign of justification. It's all through the Bible.[44]

Today it is easy to be critical of Christian churches, as I have sometimes been in this volume. Not only are they hopelessly divided among themselves, they are also susceptible to becoming subject to local loves and prejudices. And each of us as individuals has to acknowledge that we, due to our residual and often dominant self-loves, are part of the problem. Churches, we should be reminded again, are made up of sinners, saved by grace. So church communities made up of imperfect individuals are going to be imperfect communities.

Yet while we need to acknowledge our faults, those shortcomings are all the more reason to emphasize and to cultivate the beauties of Christian loves that are also manifested wherever

---

[43]Edwards, "The Duty of Charity to the Poor," *WJE* 17:400-401.

[44]Tim Keller, "If You Love Justification, You Will Love Justice," April 14, 2011, TGC 2011 National Post-Conference, Chicago, Illinois, *The Gospel Coalition Podcast*, www.thegospelcoalition.org/podcasts/tgc-podcast/love-justification-will-love -justice/. Keller, in *Generous Justice: How God's Grace Makes Us Just* (New York: Penguin Books, 2016), 68-75, summarizes Edwards's sermon on these same points.

the gospel is heard. Despite all the failures that we can acknowledge in imperfect Christians and their communities, we can also point to countless lives that have been changed in admirable ways from what they might have been otherwise. In any church setting, it is not difficult to point to beautiful aspects of loving family relationships that might have been less good without the gospel's strengthening of mutual commitments. Or we might point to the ways in which many everyday lives are enhanced by expressions of grace that might not have been as often seen otherwise in matters of honesty, integrity, concern for others, or sexual fidelity. Or think of those who, due to Christian commitments, are less likely to engage in criminal and illegal activities or to routinely alter their consciousness with drugs or alcohol. Or we consider those who are more likely to promote justice in their communities and reconciliation among contending groups. Increases in acts of charity are one of the most visible ways in which Christians grace the world. Virtually every church includes charitable programs that support the poor, the sick, the widows and orphans, and the oppressed. In the United States it is well documented that church members not only give more to charities, on average, than do their secular counterparts, but they even give more to secular charities. The same is true regarding volunteer work, or to help out a neighbor or a stranger.[45] Such instances of true virtue, while not transforming the whole world or even the whole church body, are like the beautiful crocuses that are the harbingers of the coming summer.

---

[45]Robert D. Putnam and David E. Campbell, *American Grace: How Religion Divides and Unites Us* (New York: Simon and Schuster, 2010), 444-54.

When we pray, "Your kingdom come," we should be backing our request by cultivating the small beauties that evidence our future hopes.

Cultivating such virtues in our churches is also essential to our witness to the gospel. It is an elemental principle that our message will be much more compelling if its effects can be seen in what we do and how we live.

And witnessing through the beauty of what we do and how we live is especially essential in the twenty-first century. Today we live in what is sometimes called the "post-truth" age, in which often there is no common ground for argument. Any claim can be met with a seemingly comparable counterclaim. And the stronger one's argument, the more resourceful those who disagree will be in constructing a counterargument. And people deeply committed to fundamentally opposed paradigms simply will not be open to hearing what we are saying.

Here we can learn from the great twentieth-century analyst of paradigm conflicts, Thomas Kuhn. In *The Structure of Scientific Revolutions* Kuhn famously pointed out that even the natural sciences are not wholly objective but depend on underlying premises. People with one interpretive framework are mystified by those who view the evidence through the lens of a new and incommensurable paradigm. But what then, he asks, can bring some people to nonetheless convert to a whole new outlook? What they say, he observes, is, "'I do not know how the proponents of the new view succeed, but I must learn whatever they are doing, it is clearly right.'"[46]

---

[46]Thomas Kuhn, *The Structure of Scientific Revolutions*, 2nd ed. (Chicago: University of Chicago Press, 1970), 203.

Or for Christians and Christian communities, we might hope that what observers will say is, "There is beauty in the way they live. I must learn whatever they are doing, it is clearly right."[47]

Edwards, in *Religious Affections*, offers us a comprehensive guide to what such attractive, rightly ordered loves ought to look like. They are often elusive, especially given our human skill at self-deceit. And, as Edwards found in Northampton, they are even more difficult to sustain in communities than in individuals. Still, in communities as well as in individuals, the beauty of rightly ordered loves can often shine through the clouds.

It is important to keep in mind that what must hold our lesser loves in place is our loving response to the *personal* love of God, expressed most fully in the sacrificial love of Christ and sustained by the person of the Holy Spirit. That is why Edwards begins his account of the positive signs of true love by emphasizing much the same themes as in "A Divine and Supernatural Light." That might have been called "A Divine and Supernatural Love." Being given eyes to see the light is, after all, a metaphor for having one's heart opened to recognize the beauty of God's love in Christ. And if we recognize the beauty of that love, it has a power to draw us to it. That is part of the mystery of conversion as being God's action that brings our voluntary loving response to it. We will have new sensibilities, like one who actually tastes honey, rather than just hearing it is sweet

---

[47]David Brooks, in reflecting on his own gradual conversion from atheism to Christianity, offers a nice example of what can help bring such a paradigm shift. It was, he says, largely the result of spending a lot of time visiting Christian college campuses, going to Christian conferences, and meeting with thoughtful Christian organizations. The more he did so, the more he realized that these people and communities had something that he was looking for and needed. David Brooks, "David Brooks on Faith in Polarized Times," BioLogos, May 23, 2022, https://biologos.org/resources/david-brooks-on-faith-in-polarized-times.

and delightful. If that is happening, then we should be able to recognize in ourselves evidence of the traits of the humble child of God that Edwards describes. And the culminating evidence of such loves should be seen in actual practices of our love for our neighbors, as seen in our promotion of peace and justice and especially in manifold works of charity.[48]

When Edwards speaks of "an infinite fountain of light," then, he is pointing toward the infinite beauty of the love of God at the heart of reality. We might think of it also as "an infinite fountain of love." Without that love we are lost, feeling our way in a world of dark shadows. Yet we humans are so often preoccupied with our passions and lesser loves close at hand, we fail to recognize the beauty of God's transforming love. Our natural instincts are to remain as comfortably content in the dank darkness as mushrooms. Yet we have the potential to become exquisitely wonderful flowers nourished by the sun.

---

[48]Part Three of *Religious Affections*, on the twelve positive signs, can profitably be read devotionally, though one might want to skim through some of the long argumentation. There are also two more accessible renderings: Gerald R. McDermott, *Seeing God: Twelve Reliable Signs of True Spirituality* (Downers Grove, IL: InterVarsity Press, 1995), and Sam Storms, *Signs of the Spirit: An Interpretation of Jonathan Edwards'* Religious Affections (Wheaton, IL: Crossway, 2007).

"A DIVINE AND SUPERNATURAL LIGHT" (1733)

A Sermon by Jonathan Edwards

MATTHEW 16:17

And Jesus answered and said unto him, Blessed art thou,
Simon Barjona: for flesh and blood hath not revealed
it unto thee, but my Father which is in heaven.

. . .

That there is such a thing, as a spiritual and divine light, immediately imparted to the soul by God, of a different nature from any that is obtained by natural means.[1]

. . .

I. I would show what this spiritual and divine light is. And in order to it would show,

First, in a few things what it is not. And here,

1. Those convictions that natural men may have of their sin and misery is not this spiritual and divine light. . . .

. . .

---

[1]This sermon excerpt is edited to remove an introductory section and the detail concerning what the divine light is not.

2. This spiritual and divine light don't consist in any impression made upon the imagination. . . .

3. This spiritual light is not the suggesting of any new truths, or propositions not contained in the Word of God. . . .

4. 'Tis not every affecting view that men have of the things of religion, that is this spiritual and divine light. . . .

But I proceed to show, *secondly*, positively, what this spiritual and divine light is.

And it may be thus described: a true sense of the divine excellency of the things revealed in the Word of God, and a conviction of the truth and reality of them, thence arising.

This spiritual light primarily consists in the former of these, viz. a real sense and apprehension of the divine excellency of things revealed in the Word of God. A spiritual and saving conviction of the truth and reality of these things, arises from such a sight of their divine excellency and glory; so that this conviction of their truth is an effect and natural consequence of this sight of their divine glory. There is therefore in this spiritual light,

1. A true sense of the divine and superlative excellency of the things of religion; a real sense of the excellency of God, and Jesus Christ, and of the work of redemption, and the ways and works of God revealed in the gospel. There is a divine and superlative glory in these things; an excellency that is of a vastly higher kind, and more sublime nature, than in other things; a glory greatly distinguishing them from all that is earthly and temporal. He that is spiritually enlightened truly apprehends and sees it, or has a sense of it. He don't merely rationally believe that God is glorious, but he has a sense of the gloriousness of God in his heart. There is not only a rational belief that God is holy, and

that holiness is a good thing; but there is a sense of the loveliness of God's holiness. There is not only a speculatively judging that God is gracious, but a sense how amiable God is upon that account; or a sense of the beauty of this divine attribute.

There is a twofold understanding or knowledge of good, that God has made the mind of man capable of. The first, that which is merely speculative or notional: as when a person only speculatively judges, that anything is, which by the agreement of mankind, is called good or excellent, viz. that which is most to general advantage, and between which and a reward there is a suitableness; and the like. And the other is that which consists in the sense of the heart: as when there is a sense of the beauty, amiableness, or sweetness of a thing; so that the heart is sensible of pleasure and delight in the presence of the idea of it. In the former is exercised merely the speculative faculty, or the understanding strictly so called, or as spoken of in distinction from the will or disposition of the soul. In the latter the will, or inclination, or heart, are mainly concerned.

Thus there is a difference between having an opinion that God is holy and gracious, and having a sense of the loveliness and beauty of that holiness and grace. There is a difference between having a rational judgment that honey is sweet, and having a sense of its sweetness. A man may have the former, that knows not how honey tastes; but a man can't have the latter, unless he has an idea of the taste of honey in his mind. So there is a difference between believing that a person is beautiful, and having a sense of his beauty. The former may be obtained by hearsay, but the latter only by seeing the countenance. There is a wide difference between mere speculative, rational judging anything to be excellent, and having a sense of its sweetness, and beauty. The former rests only in the head, speculation only is concerned in it; but the heart is concerned in the latter. When the heart is sensible of the beauty and amiableness of a thing, it necessarily feels pleasure in the apprehension. It is implied in a person's being heartily sensible of the loveliness of a thing, that the idea of it is sweet and pleasant to his soul; which is a far different thing from having a rational opinion that it is excellent.

2. There arises from this sense of divine excellency of things contained in the Word of God, a conviction of the truth and reality of them: and that either indirectly, or directly.

First, indirectly, and that, two ways.

1. As the prejudices that are in the heart, against the truth of divine things, are hereby removed; so that the mind becomes susceptive of the due force of rational arguments for their truth. The mind of man is naturally full of prejudices against the truth of divine things: it is full of enmity against the doctrines of the gospel; which is a disadvantage to those arguments that prove their truth, and causes them to lose their force upon the mind. But when a person has discovered to him the divine excellency of Christian doctrines, this destroys the enmity, removes those prejudices, and sanctifies the reason, and causes it to lie open to the force of arguments for their truth.

Hence was the different effect that Christ's miracles had to convince the disciples, from what they had to convince the scribes and Pharisees. Not that they had a stronger reason, or had their reason more improved; but their reason was sanctified, and those blinding prejudices, that the scribes and Pharisees were under, were removed by the sense they had of the excellency of Christ, and his doctrine.

2. It not only removes the hindrances of reason, but positively helps reason. It makes even the speculative notions the more lively. It engages the attention of the mind, with the more fixedness and intenseness to that kind of objects; which causes it to have a clearer view of them, and enables it more clearly to see their mutual relations, and occasions it to take more notice of them. The ideas themselves that otherwise are dim, and obscure, are by this means impressed with the greater strength, and have a light cast upon them; so that the mind can better judge of them. As he that beholds the objects on the face of the earth, when the light of the sun is cast upon them, is under greater advantage to discern them in their true forms, and mutual relations, than he that sees them in a dim starlight or twilight.

The mind having a sensibleness of the excellency of divine objects, dwells upon them with delight; and the powers of the soul are more awakened, and enlivened to employ themselves in the contemplation of them, and exert themselves more fully and much more to purpose. The beauty and sweetness of the objects draws on the faculties, and draws forth their exercises: so that reason itself is under far greater advantages for its proper and free exercises, and to attain its proper end, free of darkness and delusion. But,

Secondly, a true sense of the divine excellency of the things of God's Word doth more directly and immediately convince of the truth of them; and that because the excellency of these things is so superlative. There is a beauty in them that is so divine and godlike, that is greatly and evidently distinguishing of them from things merely human, or that men are the inventors and authors of; a glory that is so high and great, that when clearly seen, commands assent to their divinity, and reality. When there is an actual and lively discovery of this beauty and excellency, it won't allow of any such thought as that it is an human work, or the fruit of men's invention. This evidence, that they, that are spiritually enlightened, have of the truth of the things of religion, is a kind of intuitive and immediate evidence. They believe the doctrines of God's Word to be divine, because they see divinity in them, i.e. they see a divine, and transcendent, and most evidently distinguishing glory in them; such a glory as, if clearly seen, don't leave room to doubt of their being of God, and not of men.

Such a conviction of the truth of religion as this, arising, these ways, from a sense of the divine excellency of them, is that true spiritual conviction, that there is in saving faith. And this original of it, is that by which it is most essentially distinguished from that common assent, which unregenerate men are capable of.

II. I proceed now to the second thing proposed, viz. to show how this light is immediately given by God, and not obtained by natural means. And here,

1. 'Tis not intended that the natural faculties are not made use of in it. The natural faculties are the subject of this light: and they are the subject in such a manner, that they are not merely passive, but active in it; the acts and exercises of man's understanding are concerned and made use of in it. God in letting in this light into the soul, deals with man according to his nature, or as a rational creature; and makes use of his human faculties. But yet this light

is not the less immediately from God for that; though the faculties are made use of, 'tis as the subject and not as the cause; and that acting of the faculties in it, is not the cause, but is either implied in the thing itself (in the light that is imparted), or is the consequence of it. As the use that we make of our eyes in beholding various objects, when the sun arises, is not the cause of the light that discovers those objects to us.

2. 'Tis not intended that outward means have no concern in this affair. As I have observed already, 'tis not in this affair, as it is in inspiration, where new truths are suggested: for here is by this light only given a due apprehension of the same truths that are revealed in the Word of God; and therefore it is not given without the Word. The gospel is made use of in this affair: this light is "the light of the glorious gospel of Christ" (2 Corinthians 4:4). The gospel is as a glass, by which this light is conveyed to us; 1 Corinthians 13:12, "Now we see through a glass. . . ." But,

3. When it is said that this light is given immediately by God, and not obtained by natural means, hereby is intended, that 'tis given by God without making use of any means that operate by their own power, or a natural force. God makes use of means; but 'tis not as mediate causes to produce this effect. There are not truly any second causes of it; but it is produced by God immediately. The Word of God is no proper cause of this effect: it don't operate by any natural force in it. The Word of God is only made use of to convey to the mind the subject matter of this saving instruction: and this indeed it doth convey to us by natural force or influence. It conveys to our minds these and those doctrines; it is the cause of the notion of them in our heads, but not of the sense of the divine excellency of them in our

hearts. Indeed a person can't have spiritual light without the Word. But that don't argue, that the Word properly causes that light. The mind can't see the excellency of any doctrine, unless that doctrine be first in the mind; but the seeing the excellency of the doctrine may be immediately from the Spirit of God; though the conveying of the doctrine or proposition itself may be by the Word. So that the notions that are the subject matter of this light, are conveyed to the mind by the Word of God; but that due sense of the heart, wherein this light formally consists, is immediately by the Spirit of God. As for instance, that notion that there is a Christ, and that Christ is holy and gracious, is conveyed to the mind by the Word of God: but the sense of the excellency of Christ by reason of that holiness and grace, is nevertheless immediately the work of the Holy Spirit. I come now,

III. To show the truth of the doctrine; that is, to show that there is such a thing as that spiritual light that has been described, thus immediately let into the mind by God. And here I would show briefly, that this doctrine is both *scriptural*, and *rational*.

First, 'tis scriptural. My text is not only full to the purpose, but 'tis a doctrine that the Scripture abounds in. We are there abundantly taught, that the saints differ from the ungodly in this, that they have the knowledge of God, and a sight of God, and of Jesus Christ. I shall mention but few texts of many; 1 John 3:6, "Whosoever sinneth hath not seen him, nor known him"; 3 John 11, "He that doth good, is of God: but he that doth evil, hath not seen God"; John 14:19, "The world seeth me no more; but ye see me"; John 17:3, "And this is eternal life, that they might know thee, the only true God, and Jesus Christ whom thou hast sent." This knowledge, or sight of God and Christ, can't be a mere speculative knowledge; because it is spoken of as a seeing and knowing, wherein they differ from the ungodly. And by these scriptures it must not only be a different knowledge in degree and circumstances, and different in its effects; but it must be entirely different in nature and kind.

And this light and knowledge is always spoken of as immediately given of God; Matthew 11:25-27, "At that time Jesus answered and said, I thank thee, O Father, Lord of heaven and earth, because thou hast hid these things from the wise and prudent, and hast revealed them unto babes: even so Father; for so it seemed good in thy sight. All things are delivered unto me of my Father; and no man knoweth the Son, but the Father; neither knoweth any man the Father, save the Son, and he to whomsoever the Son will reveal him." Here this effect is ascribed alone to the arbitrary operation, and gift of God, bestowing this knowledge on whom he will, and distinguishing those with it, that have the least natural advantage or means for knowledge, even babes, when it is denied to the wise and prudent. And the imparting the knowledge of God is here appropriated to the Son of God, as his sole prerogative. And again, 2 Corinthians 4:6, "For God, who commanded the light to shine out of darkness, hath shined in our hearts, to give the light of the knowledge of the glory of God in the face of Jesus Christ." This plainly shows, that there is such a thing as a discovery of the divine superlative glory and excellency of God and Christ; and that peculiar to the saints; and also that 'tis as immediately from God, as light from the sun: and that 'tis the immediate effect of his power and will; for 'tis compared to God's creating the light by his powerful word in the beginning of the creation; and is said to be "by the

Spirit of the Lord," in the eighteenth verse of the preceding chapter [2 Corinthians 3:18]. God is spoken of as giving the knowledge of Christ in conversion, as of what before was hidden and unseen, in that [place], Galatians 1:15–16, "But when it pleased God, who separated me from my mother's womb, and called me by his grace, to reveal his Son in me . . ." The Scripture also speaks plainly of such a knowledge of the Word of God, as has been described, as the immediate gift of God; Psalms 119:18, "Open thou mine eyes, that I may behold wondrous things out of thy law." What could the Psalmist mean, when he begged of God to "open his eyes"? Was he ever blind? Might he not have resort to the law and see every word and sentence in it when he pleased? And what could he mean by those "wondrous things"? Was it the wonderful stories of the creation, and deluge, and Israel's passing through the Red Sea, and the like? Were not his eyes open to read these strange things when he would? Doubtless by "wondrous things" in God's law, he had respect to those distinguishing and wonderful excellencies, and marvelous manifestations of the divine perfections, and glory, that there was in the commands and doctrines of the Word, and those works and counsels of God that were there revealed. So the Scripture speaks of a knowledge of God's dispensation, and covenant of mercy, and way of grace toward his people, as peculiar to the saints, and given only by God; Psalms 25:14, "The secret of the LORD is with them that fear him; and he will show them his covenant."

And that a true and saving belief of the truth of religion is that which arises from such a discovery, is also what the Scripture teaches. As John 6:40, "And this is the will of him that sent me, that every one that seeth the Son, and believeth on him, may have everlasting life." Where it is plain that a true faith is what arises from a spiritual sight of Christ. And John 17:6-8, "I have manifested thy name unto the men which thou gavest me out of the world. . . . Now they have known that all things whatsoever thou hast given me are of thee; for I have given unto them the words which thou gavest me, and they have received them, and known surely that I came out from thee, and they have believed that thou didst send me." Where Christ's manifesting God's name to the disciples, or giving them the knowledge of God, was that whereby they knew that Christ's doctrine was of God, and that Christ himself was of him, proceeded from him, and was sent by him. Again, John 12:44-46, "Jesus cried and said, He that believeth on me, believeth not on me, but on him that sent me; and he that seeth me seeth him that sent me. I am come a light into the world, that whosoever believeth on me should not abide in darkness." Their believing in Christ and spiritually seeing him, are spoken of as running parallel.

Christ condemns the Jews, that they did not know that he was the Messiah, and that his doctrine was true, from an inward distinguishing taste and relish of what was divine, in Luke 12:56-57. He having there blamed the Jews, that though they could "discern the face of the sky and of the earth," and signs of the weather, that yet they could not "discern" those "times"; or as 'tis expressed in Matthew, "the signs of" those "times" [Matthew 16:3]; he adds, "Yea, and why even of your own selves judge ye not what is right?" i.e. without extrinsic signs. "Why have ye not that sense of true excellency, whereby ye may distinguish that which is holy and divine? Why have ye not that savor of the things of God, by which you may see the distinguishing glory, and evident divinity of me and my doctrine?"

The apostle Peter mentions it as what gave them (the apostles) good and well-grounded assurance of the truth of the gospel, that they had seen the divine glory of Christ; 2 Peter 1:16, "For we have not followed cunningly devised fables, when we made known unto you the power and coming of our Lord Jesus Christ, but were eyewitnesses of his majesty." The Apostle has respect to that visible glory of Christ which they saw in his transfiguration [Matthew 17:1-9]: that glory was so divine, having such an ineffable appearance and semblance of divine holiness, majesty, and grace, that it evidently denoted him to be a divine person. But if a sight of Christ's outward glory might give a rational assurance of his divinity, why may not an apprehension of his spiritual glory do so too? Doubtless Christ's spiritual glory is in itself as distinguishing, and as plainly showing his divinity, as his outward glory; and a great deal more: for his spiritual glory is that wherein his divinity consists; and the outward glory of his transfiguration showed him to be divine, only as it was a remarkable image or representation of that spiritual glory. Doubtless therefore he that has had a clear sight of the spiritual glory of Christ, may say, "I have not followed cunningly devised fables, but have been an eyewitness of his majesty," upon as good grounds as the Apostle, when he had respect to the outward glory of Christ, that he had seen. But this brings me to what was proposed next, viz. to show that,

Secondly, this doctrine is rational. 1. 'Tis rational to suppose that there is really such an excellency in divine things, that is so transcendent and exceedingly different from what is in other things, that if it were seen would most evidently distinguish them. We can't rationally doubt but that things that are divine, that appertain to the supreme Being, are vastly different from things that are human; that there is that godlike, high, and glorious excellency in them, that does most remarkably difference them from the things that are of men; insomuch that if the difference were but seen, it would have a convincing, satisfying influence upon anyone, that they are what they are, viz. divine. What reason can be offered against it? Unless we would argue that God is not remarkably distinguished in glory from men.

If Christ should now appear to anyone, as he did on the mount at his transfiguration; or if he should appear to the world in the glory that he now appears in in heaven, as he will do at the day of judgment; without doubt, the glory and majesty that he would appear in, would be such as would satisfy everyone, that he was a divine person, and that religion was true: and it would be a most reasonable, and well-grounded conviction too. And why may there not be that stamp of divinity, or divine glory on the Word of God, on the scheme and doctrine of the gospel, that may be in like manner distinguishing and as rationally convincing, provided it be but seen? 'Tis rational to suppose, that when God speaks to the world, there should be something in his word or speech vastly different from men's word. Supposing that God never had spoken to the world, but we had notice that he was about to do it; that he was about to reveal himself from heaven, and speak to us immediately himself, in divine speeches or discourses, as it were from his own mouth; or that he should give us a book of his own inditing; after what manner should we expect that he would speak? Would it not be rational to suppose, that his speech would be exceeding different from men's speech, that he should speak like a God; that is, that there should be such an excellency and sublimity in his speech or word, such a stamp of wisdom, holiness, majesty, and other divine perfections, that the word of men, yea of the wisest of men, should appear mean and base in comparison of it? Doubtless it would be thought rational to expect this, and unreasonable to think otherwise. When a wise man speaks in the exercise of his wisdom, there is something in everything he says, that is very distinguishable from the talk of a little child. So, without doubt, and much more, is the speech of God (if there be any such thing as the speech of God) to be distinguished from that of the wisest of men; agreeable to Jeremiah 23:28-29. God having there been reproving the false prophets that prophesied in his name, and pretended that what they spake was his word, when indeed it was their own word, says, "The prophet that hath a dream, let him tell a dream; and he that hath my word, let him speak my word faithfully. What is the chaff to the wheat? saith the Lord. Is not my word like as a fire? saith the Lord; and like a hammer that breaketh the rock in pieces?"

2. If there be such a distinguishing excellency in divine things, 'tis rational to suppose that there may be such a thing as seeing it. What should hinder but that it may be seen? 'Tis no argument that there is no such thing as such a distinguishing excellency, or that, if there be, that it can't be seen, that some don't see it; though they may be discerning men in temporal matters. It is not rational to suppose, if there be any such excellency in divine things, that wicked men should see it. 'Tis not rational to

suppose, that those whose minds are full of spiritual pollution, and under the power of filthy lusts, should have any relish or sense of divine beauty, or excellency; or that their minds should be susceptive of that light that is in its own nature so pure and heavenly. It need not seem at all strange, that sin should so blind the mind, seeing that men's particular natural tempers and dispositions will so much blind them in secular matters; as when men's natural temper is melancholy, jealous, fearful, proud, or the like.

3. 'Tis rational to suppose that this knowledge should be given immediately by God, and not be obtained by natural means. Upon what account should it seem unreasonable, that there should be any immediate communication between God and the creature? 'Tis strange that men should make any matter of difficulty of it. Why should not he that made all things, still have something immediately to do with the things that he has made? Where lies the great difficulty, if we own the being of a God, and that he created all things out of nothing, of allowing some immediate influence of God on the creation still? And if it be reasonable to suppose it with respect to any part of the creation, 'tis especially so with respect to reasonable intelligent creatures; who are next to God in the gradation of the different orders of beings, and whose business is most immediately with God; who were made on purpose for those exercises that do respect God, and wherein they have nextly to do with God: for reason teaches that man was made to serve and glorify his Creator. And if it be rational to suppose that God immediately communicates himself to man in any affair, it is in this. 'Tis rational to suppose that God would reserve that knowledge and

wisdom, that is of such a divine and excellent nature, to be bestowed immediately by himself, and that it should not be left in the power of second causes. Spiritual wisdom and grace is the highest and most excellent gift that ever God bestows on any creature: in this the highest excellency and perfection of a rational creature consists. 'Tis also immensely the most important of all divine gifts: 'tis that wherein man's happiness consists, and on which his everlasting welfare depends. How rational is it to suppose that God, however he has left meaner goods and lower gifts to second causes, and in some sort in their power, yet should reserve this most excellent, divine, and important of all divine communications, in his own hands, to be bestowed immediately by himself, as a thing too great for second causes to be concerned in? 'Tis rational to suppose that this blessing should be immediately from God; for there is no gift or benefit that is in itself so nearly related to the divine nature, there is nothing the creature receives that is so much of God, of his nature, so much a participation of the Deity: 'tis a kind of emanation of God's beauty, and is related to God as the light is to the sun. 'Tis therefore congruous and fit, that when it is given of God, it should be nextly from himself, and by himself, according to his own sovereign will.

'Tis rational to suppose, that it should be beyond a man's power to obtain this knowledge, and light, by the mere strength of natural reason; for 'tis not a thing that belongs to reason, to see the beauty and loveliness of spiritual things; it is not a speculative thing, but depends on the sense of the heart. Reason indeed is necessary in order to it, as 'tis by reason only that we are become the subjects of the means of it; which means I have already shown to be necessary in order to it, though they have no proper causal influence in the affair. 'Tis by reason, that we become possessed of a notion of those doctrines that are the subject matter of this divine light; and reason may many ways be indirectly, and remotely an advantage to it. And reason has also to do in the acts that are immediately consequent on this discovery: a seeing the truth of religion from hence, is by reason; though it be but by one step, and the inference be immediate. So reason has to do in that accepting of, and trusting in Christ, that is consequent on it. But if we take reason strictly, not for the faculty of mental perception in general, but for ratiocination, or a power of inferring by arguments; I say if we take reason thus, the perceiving of spiritual beauty and excellency no more belongs to reason, than it belongs to the sense of feeling to perceive colors, or to the power of seeing to perceive the sweetness of food. It is out of reason's province to perceive the beauty or loveliness of anything: such a perception don't belong to that faculty. Reason's work is to perceive truth, and not excellency. 'Tis not ratiocination that gives men the perception of the beauty and amiableness of a countenance; though it may be many ways indirectly an advantage to it; yet 'tis no more reason that immediately perceives it, than it is reason that perceives the sweetness of honey: it depends on the sense of the heart. Reason may determine that a countenance is beautiful to others; it may determine that honey is sweet to others; but it will never give me a perception of its sweetness.

I will conclude with a very brief improvement of what has been said.

First, this doctrine may lead us to reflect on the goodness of God, that has so ordered it, that a saving evidence of the truth of the gospel is such, as is attainable by persons of mean capacities, and advantages, as well as those that are of the greatest parts and learning. If the evidence of the gospel depended only on history, and such reasonings as learned men only are capable of, it would be above the reach of far the greatest part of mankind. But persons, with but an ordinary degree of knowledge, are capable, without a long and subtle train of reasoning, to see the divine excellency of the things of religion: they are capable of being taught by the Spirit of God, as well as learned men. The evidence that is this way obtained, is vastly better and more satisfying, than all that can be obtained by the arguings of those that are most learned, and greatest masters of reason. And babes are as capable of knowing these things, as the wise and prudent; and they are often hid from these, when they are revealed to those; 1 Corinthians 1:26-27, "For ye see your calling, brethren, how that not many wise men, after the flesh, not many mighty, not many noble, are called. But God hath chosen the foolish things of the world . . . ."

Secondly. This doctrine may well put us upon examining ourselves, whether we have ever had his divine light, that has been described, let into our souls. If there be such a thing indeed, and it be not only a notion, or whimsy of persons of weak and distempered brains, then doubtless 'tis a thing of great importance, whether we have thus been taught by the Spirit of God; whether the light of the glorious gospel of Christ, who is the image of God, hath shined into us, giving us the light of the knowledge of the glory of God in the face of Jesus Christ; whether we have seen the Son, and believed on him, or have that faith of gospel doctrines that arises from a spiritual sight of Christ.

Thirdly. All may hence be exhorted, earnestly to seek this spiritual light. To influence and move to it, the following things may be considered.

1. This is the most excellent and divine wisdom, that any creature is capable of. 'Tis more excellent than any human learning; 'tis far more excellent, than all the knowledge of the greatest philosophers, or statesmen. Yea, the least glimpse of the glory of God in the face of Christ doth more exalt and ennoble the soul, than all the knowledge of those that have the greatest speculative understanding in divinity, without grace. This knowledge has the most noble object that is, or can be, viz. the divine glory, and excellency of God, and Christ. The knowledge of these objects is that wherein consists the most excellent knowledge of the angels, yea, of God himself.

2. This knowledge is that which is above all others sweet and joyful. Men have a great deal of pleasure in human knowledge, in studies of natural things; but this is nothing to that joy which arises from this divine light shining into the soul. This light gives a view of those things that are immensely the most exquisitely beautiful, and capable of delighting the eye of the understanding. This spiritual light is the dawning of the light of glory in the heart. There is nothing so powerful as this to support persons in affliction, and to give the mind peace and brightness, in this stormy and dark world.

3. This light is such as effectually influences the inclination, and changes the nature of the soul. It assimilates the nature to the divine nature, and changes the soul into an image of the same glory that is beheld; 2 Corinthians 3:18, "But we all with open face beholding as in a glass the glory of the Lord, are

changed into the same image, from glory to glory, even as by the Spirit of the Lord." This knowledge will wean from the world, and raise the inclination to heavenly things. It will turn the heart to God as the fountain of good, and to choose him for the only portion. This light, and this only, will bring the soul to a saving close with Christ. It conforms the heart to the gospel, mortifies its enmity and opposition against the scheme of salvation therein revealed: it causes the heart to embrace the joyful tidings, and entirely to adhere to, and acquiesce in the revelation of Christ as our Savior; it causes the whole soul to accord and symphonize with it, admitting it with entire credit and respect, cleaving to it with full inclination and affection. And it effectually disposes the soul to give up itself entirely to Christ.

4. This light, and this only, has its fruit in an universal holiness of life. No merely notional or speculative understanding of the doctrines of religion, will ever bring to this. But this light, as it reaches the bottom of the heart, and changes the nature, so it will effectually dispose to an universal obedience. It shows God's worthiness to be obeyed and served. It draws forth the heart in a sincere love to God, which is the only principle of a true, gracious and universal obedience. And it convinces of the reality of those glorious rewards that God has promised to them that obey him.

GENERAL INDEX

SCRIPTURE INDEX